Vegetarian Cookbook:
100 – 5 Ingredients or Less Quick and Easy Vegetarian Recipes (Volume 2)

Gina 'The Veggie Goddess' Matthews

Copyright

Copyright © 2013 by Gina 'The Veggie Goddess' Matthews

Cover and internal design © by Gina 'The Veggie Goddess' Matthews

All rights reserved. No part of this book may be reproduced in any form, or by any electronic or mechanical means, including information storage and retrieval systems, except in the case of brief quotations in articles or reviews, without permission in writing from the author, Gina 'The Veggie Goddess' Matthews.

Any brand names and product names mentioned within this book are trademarks, registered trademarks, or trade names of their respective holders. The author is not associated with any product or vendor mentioned within this book.

ISBN-10: 1494289520
ISBN-13: 978-1494289522

TABLE OF CONTENTS

Introduction 1

Chapter 1 – Appetizers 5
   Cheesy Baked Wontons Crisps 7
   Greek Cucumber Dill Dip 7
   Peppery Cheese Stuffed Sugar Snap Peas 8
   Zesty Grilled Avocado Skins 9
   Salad Shells 10
   Nutty Sweet Potato Fries 11
   Veggies and Rice Sushi Rolls 13
   Mashed Potato "Meatballs" 14
   Cinnamon Chips 15
   Fancy Dried Fruit and Cheese Wheels 16
   Italian Baked Portobello Bites 17
   Mexican Fiesta Pico de Gallo Dip 19
   Pesto and Roasted Red Pepper Pinwheels 19
   Make It Sweet or Savory Hawaiian Cheese Ball 21
   Chunky Cucumber and Chive Dip 22

Chapter 2 – Soups 25
   Cheesy Broccoli Bean Chowder 27
   Tortellini and Mushroom Soup 28
   English Dilled Pea Soup 29
   White Bean and Cabbage Soup 30
   Shiitake and Tofu Soup 31
   Chili Chowder 31

Spicy Tomato Macaroni Soup *32*
Minty Leek and Sugar Snap Pea Soup *33*
Easy Thick and Chunky Southwest Soup *34*
Parmesan Asparagus Couscous Soup *35*
Light and Healthy Consomme *35*
Easy Tomato Bisque *36*
Egg Drop Soup *37*
Cold Citrus Cantaloupe Soup *38*
Creamy Zucchini Soup *39*
Classic French Onion Soup *40*
Polynesian Tomato Soup *41*
Cold Corn Soup *41*

Chapter 3 – Salads 43

Fresh Classic Italian Dinner Salad *45*
Cold Green Pea and Peanut Salad *45*
Grilled Romaine Heart Salad *46*
Sweet and Salty Orange and Olive Salad *47*
Chilled Lemon and Garlic Potato Salad *48*
Chilled Greek Orzo Spinach Salad *49*
Hawaiian Broccoli Slaw *50*
Sweet and Spicy Mango Salad *51*
Mediterranean Artichoke Heart Salad *51*
Fresh and Tangy Celery and Blue Cheese Salad *52*
Spring Salad Greens with Grapefruit and Avocado *53*
Cold Spaghetti Salad *54*
Asian Sesame Cucumber Salad *55*
Easy Marinated Fennel Apple Salad *56*
Cinnamon Honey Fruit Salad *57*
Pesto Tortellini Salad *57*
Decadent Creamy Cheesy Apple Salad *58*

Chapter 4 – Sides 61

Easy Risotto Cakes *63*
Twice Baked Blue Cheese Potatoes *64*
Super Simple Creamed Spinach *65*
Spinach and Pine Nut Quinoa *66*
Velvety Sweet Potatoes with Maple Onions *67*
Garlic and Cream Sherry Mushrooms *69*
Asiago Sweet Peppers and Asparagus *69*

Make Your Own Stove Top Stuffing Mix..........................70
Make Your Own Long Grain and Wild Rice Mix..............71
Basil Garlic Green Beans with Pine Nuts 72
Garlic and Rosemary Potatoes and Onions 73
Herbed English Yorkshire Pudding................................74
Garlic Kale with Caramelized Onions.............................75
Traditional Southern Fried Okra.....................................76
Sesame Broccoli..77
Broiled Cheesy Zucchini Rounds....................................78
Easy Potato Pancakes...79
Sweet and Tangy Roasted Carrots..................................80

Chapter 5 – Entrees..83

Baked Stuffed Portobello Caps..85
Grilled Mediterranean Pizza 86
Classic Spaghetti Genovese..87
Spinach Quiche Cups..88
Garlic Quinoa Stuffed Bell Peppers 89
Rice and Bean Burritos...91
South-of-the-Border Stuffed Poblano Peppers 92
Baked Cheesy Ziti 93
Peasant Style Mock Kielbasa and Cabbage Stew.............94
Tex Mex Casserole...95
Mock Chicken Teriyaki Stir Fry......................................96
Spinach and Cheese Stuffed Acorn Squash Bowls...........97
Spaghetti Squash "Pasta" with Garlic Butter Parmesan Sauce..98
Slow Cooker Indian Rice and Lentils 99
Greek Brunch Frittatas..100

Chapter 6 – Desserts 103

Baked Peaches and Granola...105
Easy Chocolate Mousse...106
Pecan Meringue Cookies...107
Frozen Lemon Cups..108
Vanilla Shortbread Cookies...110
Italian Balsamic Strawberries 111
Warm Banana Coconut Dessert Soup 111
Mini Pecan Pie Cupcakes..112
Nutty Chocolate Orange Fudge......................................113

Tofu Banana Split Dessert Salad 114
Italian Wedding Cookies 115
White Chocolate Lemon Bark 116
Design Your Own Dessert Crepes 117
Warm Cinnamon Dusted Orange and Apple Rings 118
Crock Pot Turtles 118
Light and Fluffy Italian Sponge Cake 120
No-Bake Nut Butter Cookie Balls 121

Bonus Chapter 1: 15 DIY Seasoning Blend Recipes 123

Easy Mediterranean Seasoning Blend 126
Southern Creole Seasoning Blend 127
Easy Garam Masala Indian Seasoning Blend 128
Cajun Seasoning Blend 128
Asian Seasoning Blend 129
Classic Herbs de Provence 130
Chili Seasoning Blend 130
Homemade Curry Powder Seasoning 131
Homemade Italian Seasoning Blend 132
Fajita Seasoning Blend 133
Creole Seasoning Blend 133
Homemade Beau Monde Seasoning Blend 134
Zesty Seasoning Salt Blend 135
Spicy Salt-Free Seasoning Blend 136
Lemon Pepper Salt Seasoning Blend 136

Bonus Chapter 2: Tips for a Successful Vegetarian Lifestyle 139

Lose the "I need to be perfect" attitude. 142
Produce prepping and repurposing leftovers. 142
Choose your kitchen appliances and gadgets wisely. 144
Don't be a junk food vegetarian. 146
Realize that your shopping habits are going to change .. 147
Avoid eating out...yes, this includes when you are at work or school. 148
Support and strengthen your vegetarian lifestyle by getting educated. 149
Don't expect those around you to support your vegetarian lifestyle. 150

Convert your favorite dishes into vegetarian versions. ..151
Transitioning, detoxing, awakening and aligning to a healthier you. 152

Available Books by Author: 155

About the Author: 163

100 – 5 Ingredients or Less Quick & Easy Vegetarian Recipes
(Volume 2)

INTRODUCTION

I have been writing vegetarian and vegan cookbooks for almost two years now, and the biggest request I get from readers of my blog, is more 5 ingredients or less recipes. Let's face it, we live in harried times and even in the best of circumstances, the time to produce healthy, home prepared meals is at a premium. And, if it's too time consuming, too complicated or too expensive, people just aren't going to follow through with their intentions to make healthier vegetarian based meals. So, I took to creating another round of quick and easy 5 ingredients or less vegetarian dishes to further expand your vegetarian menu planning, along with 2 bonus chapters to help keep you on track and further support your healthy vegetarian lifestyle.

In bonus chapter 1, I've included 15 homemade seasoning spice blends for you to create from quality herbs and spices to customize the flavors of your favorite dishes. Having these seasoning blends readily prepared offsets the need to look for this particular spice and that particular spice while cooking, thus making sure that your meal preparation is always quick and easy. Additionally, making your own seasoning blends allows you the opportunity to create high quality seasonings from high quality herbs and spices of your personal choosing, instead of using the many inferior single seasonings and seasoning blends that line the grocery store shelves today. These inferior seasonings have often been adulterated with other ingredients that are not listed on the label; have been radiated, resulting in their aromas, flavors and medicinal properties being eradicated; and have oftentimes been sitting on store shelves for months and even years before you purchase them.

In bonus chapter 2, I've included comprehensive tips for transitioning and maintaining a healthy and successful vegetarian lifestyle. These tips can be useful no matter where you fall in the spectrum of vegetarian lifestyle, from the newly transitioning vegetarian to the decades-long seasoned vegetarian.

And, as with all of my cookbooks, basic kitchen supplies are all you need. You don't need to go out and buy any special gadget or appliance to create these delicious vegetarian dishes. So, bookmark your favorite recipes and don't be afraid to make adjustments or additions to suit your own personal taste preferences or accommodate a food allergy. Vegetarian cooking is a very flexible craft that uses simple ingredients to make spectacular culinary creations.

100 – 5 Ingredients or Less Quick & Easy Vegetarian Recipes
(Volume 2)

Bon Veggie Appetit!

Gina "The Veggie Goddess" Matthews

Gina 'The Veggie Goddess' Matthews

100 – 5 Ingredients or Less Quick & Easy Vegetarian Recipes (Volume 2)

CHAPTER 1 – APPETIZERS

Gina 'The Veggie Goddess' Matthews

Cheesy Baked Wontons Crisps

(preheat oven to 350 degrees and line a large cookie sheet with parchment paper)

Ingredients:

1 package wonton wrappers

½ cup melted butter OR olive oil (or combination of both)

1/3-1/2 cup grated Parmesan cheese

Cut your wonton wrappers into strips using a sharp serrated knife. Using a basting or pastry brush, LIGHTLY brush each side of your cut wonton wrapper pieces with the melted butter (or olive oil). Arrange on a single layer on your parchment-lined cookie sheet and evenly dust with the grated Parmesan cheese. Bake on center oven rack for 5-8 minutes, or until golden and crisp. Remove from oven and serve as-is, or with your favorite vegetarian or vegan dip.

Greek Cucumber Dill Dip

Ingredients:

1 cup plain Greek yogurt (use full fat)

2 medium cucumbers (peeled – grated)

1 teaspoon fresh lemon zest + 1 tablespoon fresh

squeezed lemon juice

2-3 fresh garlic cloves (finely minced)

2 tablespoons fresh chopped dill

After you have grated the cucumber, use a few paper towels to press out the excess water. Combine the dried, grated cucumber along with all the remaining ingredients into a mixing bowl, add sea salt and black pepper to taste and stir until all ingredients are well combined. Serve with your favorite crackers, fresh cut raw veggies or pita bread. Makes approximately 1-1/2 cups of dip.

Peppery Cheese Stuffed Sugar Snap Peas

Ingredients:

½ pound sugar snap peas (strings removed)

4 ounces of goat cheese (softened to room temperature)

2 tablespoons jalapeno jelly

1 tablespoon fresh chopped parsley

1 tablespoon finely chopped pecans

Bring 4 cups of salted water to a boil in a saucepan over medium-high heat. Add in the sugar snap peas and boil until bright green, about 3 minutes. Drain and rinse under cold water. Using a sharp knife, carefully make an incision along the top seam of each pod to create a pocket.

In a small mixing bowl, stir together the room temperature goat cheese, jalapeno jelly and fresh chopped parsley until thoroughly blended. Spoon or pipe the jalapeno-cheese filling into each of the sugar snap pea pockets. Arrange the stuffed pods onto a serving platter and evenly sprinkle with the finely chopped pecans. Makes 4 servings.

Zesty Grilled Avocado Skins

(preheat indoor/outdoor grill to medium-high or set oven to broil)

*If you like potato skins, you'll love this delicious alternative.

Ingredients:

4 large, ripe avocados (halved and pits removed – leave flesh in the skins)

4 teaspoons – 4 tablespoons of chipotle OR hot sauce (adjust accordingly to desired heat level)

4 tablespoons fresh lime juice

¾-1 cup of grated Parmesan cheese (divided in half)

After you have halved the avocados and removed their pits, take a fork and rake it across the top of each avocado half to make shallow grooves in the flesh. Alternately, you can just generously pierce each avocado half with the fork prongs. This will allow the other ingredients to sink into the avocado flesh. Next, evenly drizzle the chipotle or hot sauce across each one, followed by an evenly drizzle of the fresh squeezed lime juice. Dust with sea salt and pepper to taste. Evenly top each of the 8 avocado halves with HALF of the grated Parmesan cheese. Arrange the prepped avocados on a cookie sheet and grill or broil for 2 minutes. Evenly top each of the 8 avocado halves with the remaining half of the grated Parmesan cheese and grill or broil for another 2 minutes, or until cheese is a nice golden brown. Serve as-is or with some fresh lime wedges on the side. Makes 4 servings of 2 avocado halves each.

Salad Shells

Ingredients:

1 package (16 ounces) jumbo pasta shells

1 cup diced tomatoes

1 cup peeled, diced cucumbers

½ cup chopped black olives

Braggs "Healthy Dressing" (to taste) – (may substitute with another olive oil and herb based dressing)

Bring a pot of salted water to a boil. Drop in the jumbo pasta shells and cook according to package directions. Drain, rinse and thoroughly drain again. Combine the diced tomatoes, cucumbers and black olives in a mixing bowl and drizzle in the Braggs dressing (or alternative dressing) to taste and toss to evenly coat and blend all ingredients. Stir in sea salt and black pepper to taste and give the mixture one last toss to blend. Using a spoon, stuff each of the cooked pasta shells with some of the salad mixture and arrange in a single layer in a large baking dish. Cover dish with plastic wrap and chill in the fridge for a minimum of 2-3 hours before serving. Makes 30-36 salad shells. *Serves well with a garnish of freshly chopped basil.

Nutty Sweet Potato Fries

(after prep – preheat oven to 425 degrees and line a large cookie sheet with parchment paper)

Ingredients:

4 sweet potatoes (peeled and cut into French fry sized pieces)

2 cups finely crushed pecans

½ teaspoon ground cinnamon

½ cup non-dairy milk

2 teaspoons cornstarch

Bring a large pot of salted water to a boil. Drop in the cut sweet potatoes and boil for 5 minutes. Drain into a colander and immediately plunge the colander into a large bowl of ice water. Let the sweet potatoes sit in the ice water for 30 minutes.

In a shallow dish, whisk together the crushed pecans and ground cinnamon along with sea salt and black pepper to taste. In a separate shallow dish, whisk together the non-dairy milk and cornstarch until the cornstarch is fully dissolved. Remove the sweet potato fries from the ice water and thoroughly dry them off with a clean kitchen towel or some paper towels.

Dredge the sweet potato fries first through the cornstarch mixture and then roll them through the pecan mixture. Arrange the prepped fries in a single layer on your parchment-lined cookie sheet. Do not overcrowd the fries. If you run out of room, just use a second cookie sheet. Bake on center oven rack for 10 minutes. Carefully flip the fries and then bake for another 10-15 minutes. Watch them closely at the 20 minute cooking mark, as you don't want the pecan crust to burn. Remove fries from oven and let them rest on the cookie sheet for 5-7 minutes before removing and serving. These are delicious as-is, or with your favorite dipping sauce. Makes 4-6 servings.

Veggies and Rice Sushi Rolls

(you will preferably need a sushi mat to make these, but it is possible to do a hand roll)

Ingredients:

1 medium sweet potato (peeled and cut into matchstick sized pieces)

1 package of Nori seaweed sheets

1-1/2 cups cooked and cooled brown rice

1 cup bean sprouts

½ cup pickled ginger (reserve the juice and put into a small dish)

Preheat oven to 400 degrees. Bake the matchstick sweet potato pieces for 15-20 minutes, or until fork tender. Remove from oven and allow them to cool.

For easy preparation, lay out all of your ingredients in an assembly line, preferably in the following order: 1) Cooked and cooled brown rice 2) Bean sprouts 3) Cooked and cooled sweet potato sticks 4) Pickled ginger 5) Reserved pickled ginger juice.

Lay a sheet of Nori onto your sushi mat. Press down a bit of the rice from left to right, only using the back 1/3 of the Nori sheet closest to you. Be sure to press the rice down gently, but firmly. Next, top the rice layer with a little of the bean sprouts, again from left to right. Place 1-3 cooked matchstick sweet potatoes (depending on how many you have) and then sprinkle with a little of the pickled ginger. Slowly roll up your roll, starting at the end closest to you with all of the filling contents. Stop when you are about 1/8 of an inch from the end – moisten your fingers with some of the reserved ginger juice and run it along the seam of the Nori sheet. This will help seal the roll. Finish rolling and place seam down onto a serving platter. Finish making your remaining sushi rolls using the same sequence. When you have completed making your rolls, cut them with a sharp serrated knife into bite sized pieces. Makes 4-5 sushi rolls, and each roll can be cut up into about 4-5 pieces. *Serve with fresh wasabi and Tamari or soy sauce on the side for dipping.

Mashed Potato "Meatballs"

(preheat oven to 375 degrees and LIGHTLY oil a large cookie sheet)

Ingredients:

1 pound of potatoes (I recommend Russet – peeled and cubed)

2-4 tablespoons olive oil

½ cup finely diced green onion

½-3/4 cup wheat germ

½-3/4 teaspoon paprika

Bring a large pot of salted water to a boil. Drop in the cubed potatoes and cook until the potatoes are tender. Drain, rinse and drain again very thoroughly. Transfer the cooked potatoes into a large mixing bowl and mash them together with the olive oil along with sea salt and black pepper to taste. You can mash them by hand or using an electric mixer, but make sure you mash them until there are no remaining lumps. Once the potatoes are mashed, stir in the diced green onion.

In a small mixing bowl, whisk together the wheat germ and paprika. Shape the potato mixture into small, meatball sized balls, and then roll them each through the wheat germ mixture to coat. Arrange the potato balls in a single layer onto your oiled cookie sheet and bake on center oven rack for 15-20 minutes. Remove from oven and let them rest on the cookie sheet for 5 minutes before transferring to a serving platter. I like to serve these with a toothpick stuck into each one. These are delicious as-is or with your favorite dipping sauce. Makes 8-10 servings.

Cinnamon Chips

(preheat oven to 350 degrees and lightly oil 1-2 large cookie sheets)

Ingredients:

10 flour tortillas

light oil (safflower, sunflower, grapeseed)

1 cup raw sugar

¼ cup ground cinnamon

In a mixing bowl, whisk together the raw sugar and ground cinnamon and set aside. Using a basting or pastry brush spread a coat of oil onto one side of all of the 10 tortillas. Using a pizza cutter, cut each of the tortillas into pizza shaped slices. Evenly sprinkle the oiled tortilla tops with desired amount of the sugar-cinnamon mixture. Arrange the prepped chips in a single layer onto your oiled cookie sheets, sugar-cinnamon side up. Bake on center oven rack for 5-8 minutes. Remove from oven and let the chips rest on the cookie sheet for 10-15 full minutes before transferring to a serving bowl or platter. Serve as-is or with your favorite dipping sauce. Makes 6-8 servings.

Fancy Dried Fruit and Cheese Wheels

Ingredients:

4 large flour tortillas (burrito sized)

1 package (8 ounces) cream cheese (softened to room temperature)

½-3/4 cup finely crumbled Feta cheese

6 ounces of dried fruit (cranberries, blueberries or raisins)

¼ cup finely diced green onions

Give the dried fruit a rough chop with a sharp knife, or a few quick pulses in a blender or food processor. In a mixing bowl, stir together the room temperature cream cheese with the finely crumbled Feta cheese, chopped dried fruit and diced green onions. Stir until all ingredients are well combined. Evenly spread ¼ of the mixture onto the center of each tortilla, stopping about 1 inch from the edges. Carefully roll up each of the tortillas and place them seam side down onto a plate. Cover with plastic wrap and chill in the fridge for a minimum of 2-3 hours before serving. When ready to serve, remove the tortillas from the fridge and using a sharp serrated knife cut each of the tortilla rolls into bite sized rounds. You may need to stick a toothpick through each one to keep them closed, plus the toothpick makes it easy to serve guests. Makes approximately 30-40 dried fruit and cheese wheel bites, depending on size.

Italian Baked Portobello Bites

(preheat oven to 375 degrees)

Ingredients:

4 large Portobello mushrooms (stems and inner grills removed)

olive oil

1 heaping cup shredded Mozzarella cheese

1 tablespoon Italian seasoning blend

1 large, ripe beefsteak tomato (cut into 8 thin slices or 4 thick slices)

After you've cleaned and prepped your mushrooms, drizzle a generous amount of olive oil into the center of each cap. Place on a large cookie sheet and bake on center oven rack for 10 minutes. While the mushroom caps are cooking, in a mixing bowl stir together the shredded cheese, Italian seasoning blend and a generous pinch of sea salt and black pepper. After 10 minutes, remove the mushrooms from the oven and evenly spoon the cheese mixture into each of the 4 mushroom caps. Top each mushroom cap with the tomatoes (1 thick slice each or 2 thin slices each). Next, drizzle some olive oil across the top of each mushroom and sprinkle with a little more sea salt and black pepper. Return to oven and bake for another 10-12 minutes. Remove from oven and allow the mushrooms to rest on the cookie sheet for 3-5 minutes before cutting each of the mushroom caps into quarters. Makes 16 mushroom pizza bites, about 4 servings. *You can make these more pizza style, by adding some marinara to the Portobello caps before topping with the remaining ingredients.

Mexican Fiesta Pico de Gallo Dip

Ingredients:

1 can (15 ounces) black beans (rinsed and drained)

1 cup corn

1 cup diced tomatoes

½ cup finely diced red onions

juice from 1 whole lime

Combine all of the ingredients together in a mixing bowl along with sea salt and black pepper to taste, and toss until all ingredients are well combined. Serve with cold or warm tortilla chips. *You can serve as-is, or with a sprinkle of freshly chopped cilantro on top. If you prefer a spicier pico de gallo, you can add in some freshly minced garlic and/or hot sauce to taste. Makes about 6 servings, at ½ cup each.

Pesto and Roasted Red Pepper Pinwheels

(preheat oven to 350 degrees)

Ingredients:

1 tube (8 ounces) crescent dinner rolls

1/3 cup prepared pesto sauce

1/3 cup chopped roasted red peppers

3 fresh garlic cloves (finely minced)

In a mixing bowl, stir together the pesto sauce, chopped roasted red peppers and minced garlic until mixture is well blended. Unwrap the crescent rolls and roll them out into 2 rectangles. Use your fingers to pinch and seal the dough perforations. Evenly spread the pesto mixture onto each of the 2 rectangle dough pieces, stopping about ¼ inch from the edge. Carefully roll up each of the dough pieces and then press the edges closed with your fingers. Cover with plastic wrap and chill in the fridge for 15 minutes.

Remove the dough logs from the fridge and using a sharp serrated knife, cut each of the dough logs into 8 rounds. Arrange the pesto rounds in a single layer onto an un-greased, large cookie sheet and bake on center oven rack for 14-18 minutes, or until golden brown. Remove from oven and let the pinwheels rest on cookie sheet for several minutes before transferring them to a serving platter. Makes 4 servings of 4 pinwheel bites each.

Make It Sweet or Savory Hawaiian Cheese Ball

(make the night before or the morning of before serving)

Ingredients:

2 packages (8 ounces each) cream cheese (softened to room temperature)

1 heaping cup finely diced pineapple (if using canned and not fresh, be sure to thoroughly drain all liquid first)

2 cups finely crush pecans (may also use finely crushed walnuts) – (divided)

(additional 2 ingredients if making sweet and savory)

¼ cup finely diced green bell pepper

2 tablespoons finely diced green onions

(additional 2 ingredients if making sweet)

¼ cup finely minced raisins

2 tablespoons finely grated and chopped carrots

In a mixing bowl, combine the softened cream cheese, diced pineapple and 1 cup of the crushed pecans. If making the cheese ball sweet and savory, add in the diced bell pepper and green onions along with a pinch of sea salt and stir until all ingredients are evenly coated and blended. If making the cheese ball sweet, add in the minced raisins and grated, chopped carrots (no salt) and stir until all ingredients are evenly coated and blended.

Form the mixture into a ball in the mixing bowl. Cover with plastic wrap and chill in the fridge overnight, or the morning of, before serving. When ready to serve, remove from the fridge and roll the cheese ball through the remaining 1 cup of crushed pecans (or walnuts) and serve with your favorite crackers. Makes 8 servings.

Chunky Cucumber and Chive Dip

Ingredients:

½ of a large cucumber (peeled and finely diced)

1 package (8 ounces) Neufchatal cheese (may also use cream cheese – softened to room temperature)

½ of a sweet onion (finely diced)

2 tablespoons finely diced fresh chives

1 tablespoon finely minced fresh mint leaves

In a mixing bowl, stir together the soften Neufchatal (or cream cheese), diced sweet onion, chives and mint leaves, along with sea salt and black pepper to taste. Stir until all ingredients are evenly and well combined. Once blended, add in the diced cucumbers and stir until evenly combined. Serve with your favorite crackers, pita chips or pita bread. Makes 4-6 servings.

Gina 'The Veggie Goddess' Matthews

CHAPTER 2 – SOUPS

Gina 'The Veggie Goddess' Matthews

Cheesy Broccoli Bean Chowder

Ingredients:

32 ounces vegetable broth

6 cups chopped broccoli (about 1-1/2 pounds of broccoli)

1 can (15 ounce) white beans, any variety (rinsed and drained) *equals about 1-1/4 cups cooked beans, if you are cooking your own beans

1 heaping cup shredded Cheddar cheese (regular or vegan)

Bring the broth to a boil over medium-high heat in a large saucepan. Add in the chopped broccoli, reduce heat to a low boil and cook until broccoli is just fork tender, about 6-8 minutes. Stir in the beans, along with sea salt and black pepper to taste, and cook for an additional 1-2 minutes until beans are heated through. Transfer half of the mixture into a blender along with half of the shredded cheese (1/2 cup) and puree until thick and creamy. Pour the pureed mixture back into the saucepot with the remaining half of the mixture and reheat for 2-3 minutes while stirring frequently until chowder is thick and heated through. *You can puree the entire mixture if you like, working in batches, or use a stick immersion blender instead of a blender to puree. Makes 4 servings.

Tortellini and Mushroom Soup

Ingredients:

4 cups vegetable broth

1 cup sliced mushrooms (mini bellas, crimini or shiitake work the best)

1 package (9 ounce) cheese stuffed tortellini

2 tablespoons fresh chopped parsley

fresh grated Parmesan cheese

Heat 2 tablespoons of the vegetable broth in a large saucepan over medium heat. Add in the sliced mushrooms and sauté for 3-4 minutes. Pour in the remaining vegetable broth and bring to a boil. Once boiling, add in the tortellini and cook to al dente'. Turn off heat and stir in the fresh chopped parsley along with sea salt and black pepper to taste. Ladle into individual serving bowls and dust top of each bowl with fresh grated Parmesan cheese. Makes 4 servings.

English Dilled Pea Soup

Ingredients:

12 cups vegetable broth OR water OR a mixture of each

2 pounds of shelled English peas

1/3 heaping cup of fresh chopped dill (plus more for garnish)

1 rounded teaspoon sea salt

¾ cup plain yogurt (regular or non-dairy)

Bring the 12 cups of vegetable broth (or water, or mixture of each) to a boil in a large saucepot over medium-high heat. Add in the shelled English peas and return to a boil. Boil for 1 minute and then reduce heat, cover and cook at a low simmer for 45-50 minutes. Give the peas a stir every 7-8 minutes.

Once the peas are cooked, you will puree the peas in 3 batches. Using a slotted spoon, transfer 1/3 of the peas into a blender or food processor, along with ½ cup of the cooked pea liquid, and puree until smooth. Spoon out the pureed pea mixture into a large bowl, and repeat 2 more times (1/3 of the peas and ½ cup of the cooked pea liquid for each batch). Return the bowl of pureed peas back into the saucepot with the remaining liquid and once again bring to a boil. Immediately reduce heat, leave uncovered and simmer until mixture reduces by about 1/3 in volume. This should take about 25-35 minutes. * Don't try to expedite the process by cranking up the heat. You want to cook it low and slow. Stir in the sea salt along with black pepper to taste and remove from heat. Ladle into 4-6 serving bowls and garnish with a dollop of yogurt and a sprinkle of fresh dill. Makes 4-6 servings.

White Bean and Cabbage Soup

Ingredients:

4-1/2 cups vegetable broth

2 cups rough chopped green cabbage

1 cup shredded carrots

5-6 fresh garlic cloves (minced)

1 can (15 ounce) any variety of white beans (with the liquid)

Bring the vegetable broth to a boil in a large saucepan over medium heat. Add in the cabbage, reduce heat and continue cooking at a low simmer for 20 minutes. Add in the shredded carrots and minced garlic at the 10 minute cooking mark. Add in the beans (along with the liquid) at the 15 minute cooking mark, along with sea salt and black pepper to taste. *Soup tastes best with a heavy hand of black pepper. Makes 4 servings.

Shiitake and Tofu Soup

Ingredients:

4 ounces extra-firm tofu (pressed dry and diced)

10 shiitake mushrooms (rough chopped)

32 ounces vegetable broth

4 tablespoons miso paste

6 large green onion spears (diced)

Heat 2 tablespoons of the vegetable broth in a large saucepan over medium heat. Add in the diced tofu and mushrooms and sauté for 5 minutes while stirring frequently. Pour in the remaining vegetable broth along with the miso paste, stir to blend and bring mixture to a low boil. Immediately reduce heat and simmer for 5 minutes. Remove from heat and ladle soup into 4 individual serving bowls and top with the diced green onion. Makes 4 servings.

Chili Chowder

Ingredients:

2 cups vegetable broth

1 can (10 ounce) diced tomatoes with green chiles (drained)

2 cans (15 ounce each) black beans (with liquid)

2 cups corn kernels

2-4 teaspoons chili seasoning blend (or to taste)

Combine all ingredients into a large saucepot and bring to a boil over medium heat. Let boil for 1-2 minutes, reduce heat to low and simmer for 10-15 minutes to allow chowder to thicken a bit. Remove from heat and ladle into individual serving bowls. Serve as-is or with your favorite toppings, such as sour cream, shredded cheese, corn chips and fresh lime wedges. Makes 4-6 servings.

Spicy Tomato Macaroni Soup

Ingredients:

2 cups dry macaroni noodles

1 large yellow onion (rough diced)

5 cups vegetable broth

32 ounces organic vegetable juice (I personally use Lakewood brand "Super Veggie")

1 tablespoon of your favorite table seasoning blend (Mrs. Dash blends are perfect for this recipe)

Bring the 5 cups of vegetable broth along with a pinch of sea salt to a boil in a large saucepan over medium heat. Add in the macaroni noodles and diced onion and cook at a low boil until pasta is al dente`, about 6-8 minutes (check package for cooking times). Stir a few times during cooking so that the noodles don't stick to the bottom of the pan. Do NOT drain. Add in the vegetable juice and table seasoning blend and return to a low boil. Cook at a low boil for 3-4 minutes and then remove from heat. Stir in sea salt and black pepper to taste and serve. Makes 4-6 servings.

Minty Leek and Sugar Snap Pea Soup

Ingredients:

32 ounces vegetable broth

¾ cup sugar snap peas (strings removed and rough chopped)

3 tablespoons chopped leeks (the green part only)

3 tablespoons butter (unsalted)

1-2 tablespoons freshly chopped mint leaves (divided)

Combine all of the ingredients (reserving half of the freshly chopped mint) in a saucepan and bring to a low boil over medium heat. Cook at a boil for 1-2 minutes, reduce heat and simmer until the vegetables are fork-tender. Turn off heat and carefully ladle out half of the soup mixture into a blender or food processor and puree until smooth. Pour the puree back into the saucepan, stir to blend and reheat on medium-low until soup is heated through. Ladle into serving bowls and evenly top each one with the remaining fresh chopped mint. Makes 4 servings.

Easy Thick and Chunky Southwest Soup

Ingredients:

2 cups corn kernels

2 cans (15 ounces each) black beans (do not drain)

1 can (10 ounces) Ro*Tel diced tomatoes with green chilies (with liquid)

1-2 teaspoons powdered chili seasoning

shredded Mexican or Colby cheese

This is a super easy, super fast supper to make when you are time-crunched. Combine all of the ingredients (except the cheese) in a saucepan over medium heat. Remember to retain the liquid from both the beans and the diced tomatoes-green chilies. Stir to blend and cook for 10 minutes, while stirring occasionally. Ladle into 4 individual soup bowls and top with desired amount of shredded cheese. Makes 4 servings. Soup serves well with a salad and some warm or cold tortilla chips or bread.

100 – 5 Ingredients or Less Quick & Easy Vegetarian Recipes (Volume 2)

Parmesan Asparagus Couscous Soup

Ingredients:

3 cups vegetable broth

1 cup dry couscous

1 bunch of fresh asparagus (ends trimmed and cut into 1 inch pieces)

freshly grated Parmesan cheese (to taste)

Bring the vegetable broth to a boil in a saucepan over medium heat. Stir in the couscous, return to a boil and let cook at a boil for a full 5 minutes. Add in the chopped asparagus, again return to a boil, and continue to cook at a boil for another 4 minutes. Remove from heat, at sea salt and black pepper to taste and let the soup sit for 5 minutes in the saucepan. Add this point you can either add desired amount of freshly grated Parmesan cheese to the saucepan and stir to blend, or ladle the soup into 4 individual soup bowls and add desired amount of the freshly grated Parmesan cheese to the top of each bowl, and then serve. Makes 4 servings.

Light and Healthy Consomme

Ingredients:

4 cups vegetable broth

1 ripe avocado (peeled, pitted and cut into cubes)

1 lemon (peeled, seeded and cut into small rough diced sized pieces)

4 tablespoons sherry (you can substitute with equal amount of a dry white wine)

¼ cup fresh chopped parsley

Evenly divide the cubed avocado and diced lemon pieces into the bottom of 4 individual soup bowls. Pour 1 tablespoon of sherry (or dry white wine) onto the top of the avocados and lemons in each bowl. In a saucepan over medium heat, bring the vegetable broth to a low boil. Immediately remove from heat and evenly pour about 1 cup of broth into each of the serving bowls. Sprinkle the chopped parsley onto the top of each bowl and serve. Makes 4 servings.

Easy Tomato Bisque

Ingredients:

4 cups diced tomatoes

1 cup heavy cream

2-3 teaspoons Italian seasoning blend

2 fresh garlic cloves (minced)

freshly chopped basil (to taste)

Combine the diced tomatoes and heavy cream in a

saucepan and bring to a low boil over medium heat. Stir in the Italian seasoning blend and minced garlic. Reduce heat and simmer for 5 minutes. Add sea salt and black pepper to taste and ladle bisque into 4 individual serving bowls. Top each with some freshly chopped basil and serve. Makes 2-4 servings. *If you prefer your bisque a little on the smoother side, you can use a stick immersion blender to puree to desired consistency.

Egg Drop Soup

Ingredients:

4 cups vegetable broth

½-3/4 cup green peas

2-3 fresh garlic cloves (minced)

3 large eggs (slightly beaten)

5-6 large green onion stalks (diced)

Add the vegetable broth along with sea salt and black pepper to taste in a saucepan, and bring to a boil over medium-high heat. Reduce heat slightly and stir in the green peas and minced garlic. Cook at a simmer for 2-3 minutes. Next, slowly pour in the lightly beaten eggs into the simmering liquid while stirring with a fork. The eggs will start to form cooked "shreds". Turn off heat and stir in the diced green onion. Let the soup sit for several minutes before serving. Makes 4 servings. *If you'd like to kick up the soup flavors a notch, you can make it with one or more of these optional add-ins: finely grated ginger root; red pepper flakes; Chinese hot pepper sauce.

Cold Citrus Cantaloupe Soup

Ingredients:

1 medium-large cantaloupe (peeled, seeded and cut into cubes)

2 cups fresh squeezed orange juice

1 tablespoon fresh squeezed lime juice

½ teaspoon ground cinnamon

freshly chopped mint leaves (for garnish)

Combine all of the ingredients (EXCEPT for the mint leaves) in a blender or food processor and puree until smooth. Transfer to fridge and chill for a minimum of 3 hours. When ready to serve, ladle into 4 individual serving bowls and top each with some of the freshly chopped mint leaves. Makes 4 servings.

Creamy Zucchini Soup

Ingredients:

4 cups vegetable broth (divided)

4 cups peeled, diced zucchini

1 large yellow onion (diced)

4 fresh garlic cloves (minced)

1 package (8 ounces) Neufchatel cheese (may substitute with cream cheese – softened to room temperature)

Bring 1 cup of the vegetable broth to a boil in a saucepan over medium heat. Add in the diced zucchini and onion, reduce heat and simmer until zucchini is fork tender. Stir in the minced garlic and Neufchatel cheese and stir continuously until the cheese has fully melted. Carefully pour the mixture into a blender and puree until smooth, or to desired consistency. (You may alternately use a stick immersion blender.) Return the pureed mixture to the saucepan along with the remaining 3 cups of vegetable broth and bring mixture to a low simmer. Simmer for about 5 minutes, or until soup is thoroughly heated through. Season with sea salt and black pepper as desired and serve. Makes 4-6 servings.

Classic French Onion Soup

(preheat oven to broil – you will need 6 ovenproof soup crocks)

Ingredients:

6 cups vegetarian "mock" beef broth (I use Edward & Sons vegan "Not Beef" bouillon cubes – 3 cubes to 6 cups of water to equal 6 cup of "mock" beef broth.)

1-1/2 cups thinly sliced white or yellow onions

4 ounces shredded Mozzarella cheese

6 slices of toasted French bread (Be sure to cut each as needed to fit into the soup crocks after toasting.)

Combine the "mock" beef broth and sliced onions along with a generous pinch of sea salt and black pepper in a saucepan, and bring to a simmer. Continue simmering for 20-25 minutes.

Arrange your soup crocks on a large cookie sheet. Evenly ladle the soup mixture into the 6 soup crocks. Place a piece of toasted French bread into each crock and top with some of the shredded Mozzarella cheese. Carefully transfer the sheet of soup crocks into the oven and broil until the cheese is bubbly and golden brown. Makes 6 servings.

Polynesian Tomato Soup

Ingredients:

8 ounces plain tomato sauce

2 tablespoons raw sugar

1 tablespoon cornstarch

1-1/2 cups unsweetened coconut milk (use the thick kind in a can)

1 tablespoon freshly grated ginger root

Combine all of the ingredients in a saucepan and bring to a low boil over medium heat while stirring frequently. Immediately reduce heat, add sea salt and black pepper to taste, and cook at a simmer for 5 minutes. Makes 2-3 servings. *Serves well with some fresh lime wedges to squeeze into the soup.

Cold Corn Soup

Ingredients:

2 cups corn kernels (if not using fresh, ok to use frozen/thawed but I don't recommend canned)

2 cups plain non-dairy milk

pinch of cayenne pepper

pinch of ground cinnamon

Combine all of the ingredients in a blender and puree until smooth. Transfer to fridge and chill for a minimum of 2 hours before serving. Add sea salt and black pepper to taste right before serving. Makes 2 servings.

100 – 5 Ingredients or Less Quick & Easy Vegetarian Recipes
(Volume 2)

CHAPTER 3 – SALADS

Gina 'The Veggie Goddess' Matthews

Fresh Classic Italian Dinner Salad

*Italians have a handful of classic dinner salad variations, and this is one of my favorites!

Ingredients:

2 medium sized cucumbers (peeled and diced)

1 pint of cherry tomatoes (halved)

½ of a red onion (sliced into thin half rings)

olive oil

balsamic vinegar

Combine the diced cucumbers, halved cherry tomatoes and sliced red onions in a mixing bowl and drizzle in olive oil and balsamic vinegar to taste. Add sea salt and black pepper if desired and toss to evenly coat and combine all ingredients. Makes 4 servings.

Cold Green Pea and Peanut Salad

Ingredients:

¾ cup mayonnaise (regular or vegan)

2 tablespoons finely diced red onion (may also use diced green onion)

1 tablespoon fresh squeezed lemon juice

2 cups cooked green peas

10 ounces roasted peanuts (may also use honey roasted nuts for a slighter sweeter flavor)

In a mixing bowl, stir together the mayonnaise, diced onion and lemon juice until well blended. Cover and chill in the fridge for 1 hour. Remove dressing from the fridge and add in the 2 cups of cooked green peas and roasted peanuts. Toss to evenly coat and blend all ingredients and add in sea salt and black pepper to taste. Serve immediately. Makes 4 servings.

Grilled Romaine Heart Salad

Ingredients:

2 large Romaine Hearts (halved lengthwise through the core to make 4 sections)

1 large orange (peeled – halved)

4 large green onion spears (rough diced)

olive oil

¼ cup finely crumbled Blue Cheese (may substitute with finely crumbled Feta cheese)

In a small mixing bowl, squeeze the juice from 1 half of the halved orange. Add in 2 tablespoons of olive oil and whisk to blend. Segment and rough chop the other half of the orange and set aside.

Preheat a large skillet over high heat. LIGHTLY brush one side of each of the 4 sections of Romaine hearts with olive oil. (*Be carefully to not over-oil, otherwise you'll end up with soggy Romaine hearts.) Once your skillet is preheated, arrange your Romaine hearts in a single layer and grill for 1 minute on each side until it just starts to wilt. This may take slightly less time depending on how hot your skillet is.

Remove the grilled Romaine hearts and arrange either on one large serving platter or 4 individual serving plates. Sprinkle evenly with the rough chopped orange pieces, diced green onion and crumbled Blue Cheese. Lastly, give each a drizzle with the orange juice infused olive oil and sea salt and black pepper to taste. Makes 2-4 servings.

Sweet and Salty Orange and Olive Salad

Ingredients:

1 head of Boston lettuce (hand torn into bite sized pieces)

2 navel oranges + the zest from 1 of the oranges (peeled, seeded and segmented – be sure to remove all of the white pithy part)

1 small red onion (rough chopped)

½ cup sliced black olives

Vinaigrette dressing, to taste (I use Braggs "Healthy Vinaigrette")

Arrange the torn Boston lettuce pieces onto one large serving platter, or divide it up onto between 4-6 small individual serving plates.

Combine the zest from 1 of the oranges, along with the orange segments, chopped onion and sliced black olives in a mixing bowl. Sprinkle in sea salt and black pepper to taste along with desired amount of vinaigrette dressing. (I use between 1/3-1/2 of a cup) Toss to evenly coat and blend ingredients and then evenly spread the salad ingredients onto the top of your torn Boston lettuce pieces. Makes 4-6 servings.

Chilled Lemon and Garlic Potato Salad

Ingredients:

2-1/2 pounds red potatoes (washed and cubed)

fresh squeezed juice from 2 large lemons (plus zest from 1 lemon for garnish – optional)

1 tablespoon light oil (sunflower, safflower, grapseed, etc.)

3 cloves of fresh garlic (finely minced)

½ cup of fresh chopped parsley

Bring a large pot of salted water to a boil. Drop in

the cubed potatoes and boil until fork tender. Drain thoroughly. In a large mixing bowl, stir together the lemon juice, oil, minced garlic and chopped parsley. Add in the cooked, cubed potatoes and toss until potatoes are all evenly coated and blended with the other ingredients. Add sea salt and black pepper to taste, and toss again to blend. Cover bowl and chill in the fridge for a minimum of 3 hours before serving. Serve with an optional garnish of freshly grated lemon zest on top. Makes 4-6 servings.

Chilled Greek Orzo Spinach Salad

Ingredients:

1 package (16 ounces) orzo pasta

5-6 heaping cups hand torn baby spinach

1 can pitted black olives (sliced)

4 ounces finely crumbled Feta cheese (you may substitute with finely crumbled Blue Cheese)

6-8 ounces of Braggs Healthy Salad Dressing (you may substitute with another healthy brand of dressing that includes olive oil-apple cider vinegar-herbs)

Cook the orzo pasta according to package directions, drain and cool. Once cooled, combine the orzo in a mixing bowl along with all of the remaining ingredients and toss to evenly coat and blend all ingredients. Chill for a minimum of 1 hour before serving. Makes 6-8 servings.

Hawaiian Broccoli Slaw

Ingredients:

1 bag (12 ounces) broccoli slaw mix

1-1/4 cups diced pineapple (if using canned pineapple, be sure to thoroughly rinse and drain first)

½ cup raisins (dark or golden)

½ cup chopped nuts (walnuts, pecans or almonds)

Braggs "Hawaiian Dressing" (about 6-8 ounces, or to taste)

Combine all of the ingredients in a large mixing bowl and toss to evenly coat and blend all ingredients. Cover and chill in the fridge for a minimum of 1 hour before serving. This salad is sturdy enough to make several hours, or even the same day morning of, before serving. Makes 4-6 servings.

Sweet and Spicy Mango Salad

Ingredients:

4 large, ripe mangos (peeled and diced)

a small handful of fresh mint leaves (rough chopped)

2 tablespoons of fresh chopped cilantro

½ teaspoon of chili sauce (can substitute with hot sauce or red pepper flakes to taste)

Combine all of the ingredients in a large mixing bowl and toss to evenly coat and blend all ingredients. Can be served immediately or kept chilled in the fridge until ready to serve. Makes 4 servings. *Do not substitute the fresh herbs (mint and cilantro) with their dried counterpart, as the results will not be the same.

Mediterranean Artichoke Heart Salad

Ingredients:

1 jar (14 ounces) artichoke hearts (drained and rough chopped)

1 large, ripe beefsteak tomato (seeded and diced)

½ cup of diced bell pepper (green, yellow, orange or red)

1/3 cup of diced red onion

¼ cup Braggs "Healthy Dressing" blend (you may substitute with another brand that has an olive oil and apple cider vinegar base with herbs)

Combine all of the ingredients in a large mixing bowl and toss to evenly coat and blend all ingredients, and season with sea salt and black pepper to taste. Can be served immediately or chilled in the fridge until ready to serve (serve within 3 hours). Makes 2-4 servings.

Fresh and Tangy Celery and Blue Cheese Salad

Ingredients:

8 large, thick celery stalks (ends trimmed and cut into 1 inch pieces)

1/3 cup diced red onions

¾ cup finely crumbled Blue Cheese (may substitute with Feta cheese)

1 tablespoon olive oil (or more, to taste)

fresh lemon wedges

Combine the celery pieces, diced red onions and crumbled Blue cheese in a mixing bowl. Drizzle in the 1 tablespoon of olive oil and toss to blend and evenly coat. At this point, if you desire a little extra olive oil, drizzle it in now along with black pepper to taste and toss again to blend. (*I don't recommend adding in any sea salt because both the celery and Blue cheese have a natural saltiness to them.) Transfer the salad into 4-6 individual serving bowls (or plates) and serve each with a fresh lemon wedge. Some people will prefer the salad with a drizzle of fresh lemon juice, while others will prefer it without. Makes 4-6 servings.

Spring Salad Greens with Grapefruit and Avocado

Ingredients:

2 cups spring salad mix

2 ripe avocados (peeled, pitted and cut into thin wedge slices)

1 large pink grapefruit (peeled, seeded and cut into thin wedge slices)

½ cup red onions (cut into thin half ring slices)

Braggs "Healthy Dressing" blend (may substitute with another healthy olive oil and herb based dressing)

Evenly divide and arrange the spring salad mix onto 4 individual serving plates. Evenly divide and arrange the avocado slices and grapefruit slices onto each plate in a circle. Evenly divide and sprinkle the red onion onto each salad plate, sprinkle with desired amount of sea salt and black pepper and serve with dressing on the side. This particular salad combination should not be prepared by tossing all the ingredients together in a mixing bowl, and the dressing is best served drizzled on top immediately before eating. Makes 4 servings.

Cold Spaghetti Salad

Ingredients:

8 ounces dry measurement (half of a pound bag or box) spaghetti noodles

½ cup diced vegetables (choose from: diced raw zucchini; diced raw mushrooms; chopped marinated artichoke hearts; or lightly cooked and diced asparagus)

¼ cup diced green onions

2-3 fresh garlic cloves (minced)

6 ounces of Braggs "Healthy Dressing" blend (you may substitute with another healthy olive oil and herb blend)

Break up the dry spaghetti into small pieces. Bring a large pot of salted water to a boil. Add in the dry spaghetti noodles pieces and cook to al dente' according to package directions. Drain, rinse and drain again. Combine the cooked spaghetti noodle pieces into a large mixing bowl along with all of the remaining ingredients, and toss to evenly coat and blend all ingredients. Cover and chill in the fridge for a minimum of 3 hours before serving. You can even make this the night before. Makes 4-6 servings.

Asian Sesame Cucumber Salad

Ingredients:

2 large cucumbers (peeled and cut into very thin slices – a mandolin slicer works great for this)

1 teaspoon sea salt

2-3 teaspoons Braggs liquid aminos (may substitute with Tamari)

1 to 1-1/2 tablespoons rice wine vinegar

1 tablespoon roasted sesame seeds

Put the thinly sliced cucumbers onto a large plate or shallow baking dish and sprinkle evenly with the 1 teaspoon of sea salt. Toss to evenly coat the cucumber with the sea salt and let sit at room temperature for 1 hour. After 1 hour, roll up the cucumber slices in batches into paper towels and gently squeeze out the briny liquid.

Next, combine the prepped cucumbers in a mixing bowl along with all of the remaining ingredients and toss to evenly coat and blend all ingredients. Start with the lesser called for amount of the liquid aminos and rice wine vinegar, taste after mixing, and add more of either ingredients as desired. Can be served immediately or chilled in the fridge until ready to serve. *You may alternately make this salad with a drizzle of roasted sesame oil in place of the sesame seeds. Makes 4 servings.

Easy Marinated Fennel Apple Salad

Ingredients:

1 large fennel bulb (stem and fronds removed)

½ of a large apple (peeled and very thinly sliced into matchstick sized pieces)

1 tablespoon fresh squeezed lemon juice

¼ cup olive oil

Slice the fennel bulb as thinly as you can, and discard the inner bulb. In a mixing bowl, whisk together the fresh squeezed lemon juice along with sea salt and black pepper to taste. Continue whisking as you then drizzle in the olive oil. Add in the sliced fennel and apple and toss to evenly coat and blend all ingredients. Cover and chill in fridge for a minimum of 3 hours before serving. Salad can also be made the night before. Makes 2-4 servings.

Cinnamon Honey Fruit Salad

Ingredients:

2 large, ripe bananas (peeled and diced)

1 large, red variety apple (peeled and diced)

1 large, sweet orange (peeled, seeded and diced)

3 tablespoons of raw honey (slightly warmed)

1 teaspoon ground cinnamon

Whisk together the warmed raw honey and ground cinnamon in a mixing bowl until well blended. Add in all of the diced fruit and toss to evenly blend and coat. Serve immediately at room temperature, or keep chilled in the fridge until ready to serve. This salad can be made several hours in advance, or the morning of, before serving. Makes 4 servings.

Pesto Tortellini Salad

Ingredients:

1 package cheese tortellini

4 ripe Roma tomatoes (seeded and diced)

1 cup cubed mozzarella cheese

½ cup prepared pesto sauce

¼ cup fresh chopped basil

Cook the cheese tortellini according to package directions, drain and rinse under cold water. Combine the cooked tortellini along with all the remaining ingredients in a large mixing bowl, and toss to evenly coat and blend all ingredients. Season with sea salt and black pepper to taste, and chill in the fridge for a minimum of 3 hours before serving. When ready to serve, allow salad to rest at room temperature for 15 minutes before serving. Makes 4 servings.

Decadent Creamy Cheesy Apple Salad

Ingredients:

5 red variety apples (peeled, seeded and cubed)

1/3 cup sour cream

4 tablespoons raw honey

2 teaspoons brown sugar

freshly shaved or shredded Sharp Cheddar cheese

In a mixing bowl, whisk together the sour cream, raw honey and brown sugar until mixture is creamy and well blended. Add in the cubed apples and toss to evenly coat and blend all ingredients. Cover and chill in the fridge for 1 hour. Salad can also be left in fridge until ready to serve. When ready to serve, evenly divide the salad onto 4 individual serving plates and top each one with some freshly shaved or shredded Sharp Cheddar cheese. (Don't substitute another type of Cheddar for this recipe, as you need the 'bite' of the Sharp Cheddar to balance out the flavors.) Makes 4 servings.

Gina 'The Veggie Goddess' Matthews

CHAPTER 4 – SIDES

Gina 'The Veggie Goddess' Matthews

Easy Risotto Cakes

*This is a great use for leftover risotto.

Ingredients:

1 extra large egg (well beaten)

2 cups leftover risotto (should be cold when starting this recipe)

1 cup breadcrumbs (plain or seasoned – divided)

1 tablespoon olive oil (divided)

Combine the beaten egg, the cooked cold risotto and ½ cup of the breadcrumbs in a mixing bowl. Stir until all ingredients are well combined. Spread the remaining ½ cup of breadcrumbs in a shallow bowl. Shape the risotto mixture into 8 - 2 inch sized balls and dredge each one thoroughly through the remaining breadcrumbs to coat and then flatten slightly with your fingers.

Heat half of the oil in a large skillet over medium heat. Add in the prepared risotto cakes and cook for 3-4 minutes until bottom is golden brown. Flip the risotto cakes over and drizzle in the remaining olive oil. Cook for an additional 3-4 minutes until other side is also golden brown. Watch so that your pan doesn't get too hot, and reduce heat if necessary to medium-low. Makes 4 servings, of 2 risotto cakes each. Your risotto cakes serve well with grilled or fried seitan steaks, veggie meatballs, or as a unique and delicious topping to a warm spinach salad.

Twice Baked Blue Cheese Potatoes

(preheat oven to broil midway through prep time – grease bottom of a shallow 8 cup baking dish)

Ingredients:

6 large golden potatoes (peeled and cubed)

6 tablespoons butter (unsalted – regular or vegan)

4 fresh garlic cloves (finely minced)

1 tablespoon fresh chopped rosemary (or 1-1/2 tablespoons of dried rosemary)

1-1/3 cups finely crumbled Blue Cheese (you can substitute with Sharp Cheddar if you don't like or have Blue Cheese)

Bring a large pot of salted water to a boil. Add in the diced potatoes and cook until they are fork tender.

While the potatoes are boiling, melt the butter in a saucepan over medium-low heat, once melted, whisk in the minced garlic and rosemary. Reduce heat to warm and allow the flavors of the seasoned butter mixture to build while the potatoes are cooking. Once the potatoes are ready, drain, rinse and drain again very thoroughly. At this time, preheat your oven to BROIL.

Transfer the cooked potatoes into a large mixing bowl and using an electric mixer beat the potatoes until they are creamy and without any lumps. Next, stir in the seasoned butter mixture along with 1 cup of the cheese until well incorporated. Season the potatoes with sea salt and black pepper to taste, spread the potato mixture into your prepared baking dish and then evenly sprinkle the remaining 1/3 cup of cheese across the top. Once your oven is preheated, broil the potatoes until the cheese is melted and golden brown, about 3-5 minutes. Remove from oven and let the potatoes rest for 5 minutes before serving. Makes 4 servings.

Super Simple Creamed Spinach

Ingredients:

2 pounds of fresh spinach (regular spinach or baby spinach)

1 cup heavy cream

If using regular spinach, make sure you have removed all of the stems. This does not have to be done with baby spinach.

Place the washed spinach into a large dry saucepan over medium heat, cover and heat just until the spinach is wilted, about 2 minutes. Remove spinach from the saucepan and onto a large cutting board, and give the spinach a quick rough chop. Press down on the chopped spinach with a couple paper towels to remove all excess water.

Heat the heavy cream in the same saucepan over

medium-low heat and bring to a low simmer. Once the cream has reached a simmer, add in sea salt and black pepper to taste, reduce heat further and simmer for 4-5 minutes to thicken and reduce. Add in the chopped spinach, stir to blend and heat for an additional 2-3 minutes. Adjust sea salt and black pepper as needed again at this point and serve. Makes 4 servings.

Spinach and Pine Nut Quinoa

Ingredients:

1 cup dry quinoa

1 large handful of fresh baby spinach (rough chopped)

2 tablespoons finely diced red bell pepper (may also use yellow or orange bell pepper)

½ cup of roasted pine nuts

2-3 tablespoons of lemon-infused olive oil

Combine the 1 cup of dry quinoa with 1-1/2 cups of water in a medium sized saucepan, and bring to a boil over medium heat. Cover pan and allow quinoa to boil for 1-2 minutes. Reduce heat to very low, keep lid on pan and continue cooking for 15 minutes. Remove pan from heat but keep the lid on, and let the quinoa sit for 5-7 minutes.

Remove lid and fluff the quinoa thoroughly with a

fork. Stir in the chopped spinach, diced bell peppers and pine nuts. Drizzle in the lemon-infused olive oil along with sea salt and black pepper to taste, and toss until all ingredients are evenly coated and well combined. Makes 4 servings. *If you don't have, or can't find, lemon-infused olive oil, simple use the called for amount of regular olive oil and squeeze in the juice from ¼ of a large lemon, or to taste.

Velvety Sweet Potatoes with Maple Onions

(preheat oven to 375 degrees)

Ingredients:

4 extra large sweet potatoes (peeled and cubed)

¼ cup +2 tablespoons real maple syrup (divided - any grade)

4 tablespoons olive oil (divided)

2-1/2 tablespoons butter

1 large sweet onion (cut into very thin slices)

Combine the cubed sweet potatoes, ¼ cup of the maple syrup, 2 tablespoons of the olive oil along with sea salt and black pepper in a mixing bowl and toss until all ingredients are evenly coated. (I recommend at least 1-1/2 teaspoons of sea salt and at least ¾ teaspoon of black pepper.) Arrange the seasoned potatoes in a single layer onto a large cookie sheet and bake on center oven rack for 30-40 minutes, stirring every 15 minutes until the potatoes are soft.

While the potatoes are baking, melt the butter and the remaining 2 tablespoons of olive oil in a saucepan over medium heat. Once melted, add in the remaining 2 tablespoons of maple syrup and the sliced onions and cook until the onions become a deep golden brown. *If saucepan becomes dry, drizzle in a little bit of water. Once the onions are caramelized, remove from heat.

When the both the potatoes and onions are done cooking, transfer in batches into a food processor and puree to desired consistency. (Alternately, you can use a stick immersion blender and puree the potatoes and onion together in a large saucepan.) Once you have the potatoes and onions pureed, return mixture to saucepan over medium heat and add sea salt and black pepper to taste. *The addition of sea salt and black pepper at this point will really make the flavors 'pop' against the sweetness of the maple caramelized onions. Stir well and cook over medium heat until potatoes are heated through. Makes 6-8 servings.

Garlic and Cream Sherry Mushrooms

Ingredients:

1-1/2 pounds mushrooms (sliced or quartered)

1 tablespoon olive oil

1/3 cup cream sherry (or more, to taste)

4 large garlic cloves (minced)

2 teaspoons fresh squeezed lemon juice

Heat the olive oil in a large skillet over medium heat. Once heated, add in the mushrooms and sauté while stirring frequently for 5-7 minutes. Add in the cream sherry and minced garlic and continue to cook and stir until almost all of the liquid has been absorbed or evaporated, about 10-12 minutes. Turn off heat and stir in the lemon juice along with sea salt and black pepper to taste. Makes 4-6 servings.

Asiago Sweet Peppers and Asparagus

Ingredients:

1 pound of fresh asparagus (ends trimmed)

1 large red, yellow or orange bell pepper (seeded and cut into thin strips)

2 tablespoons olive oil

2 teaspoons lemon-pepper seasoning blend

¼-1/3 cup freshly grated Asiago cheese

Bring a pot of salted water to a boil over medium heat. Add in the asparagus and flash cook for 2 minutes. Drain and rough chop. Heat the olive oil in a skillet over medium heat-high heat. Once heated, add in the chopped asparagus and bell pepper and sauté until crisp-tender, about 3 minutes. Add in the lemon-pepper seasoning blend and stir to evenly blend. Transfer the vegetables to a serving bowl and evenly sprinkle the grated Asiago cheese on top. Makes 4 servings. *I like to serve this with a garnish of fresh lemon wedges.

Make Your Own Stove Top Stuffing Mix

Ingredients:

6 thick slices of stale bread (preferably French or Sourdough)

1/3 heaping cup of finely chopped nuts (walnuts or pecans)

3 tablespoons Italian seasoning blend

½ teaspoon ground fennel seed (if you only have whole fennel seeds, grind them up first in a spice grinder or coffee grinder OR put the fennel seeds in a baggie and roll over with a rolling pin to crush)

1/4 teaspoon sea salt

Cut the slices of stale bread into cubes and arrange in a single layer onto 1 or 2 large cookie sheets (no oil). Dry the bread crumbs in a 250 degree oven for 50-60 minutes. Remove from oven and let cool.

Once the bread cubes have cooled, toss them into a large mixing bowl with all the remaining ingredients and toss to blend. You can now use this stuffing mixture immediately to make your stuffing, or keep it in a tightly sealed Ziploc baggie and use it within 30 days.

To make the stuffing, bring 1 cup of water to a boil in a saucepan. Turn off heat and stir in the entire stuffing mix. Stir thoroughly to ensure all of the ingredients become moistened. (*You may need to adjust the amount of water and drizzle in a little extra if mixture is too dry.) Cover the saucepan and let it sit for 5-7 minutes. Remove cover and fluff the stuffing with a fork. Makes 4 servings.

Make Your Own Long Grain and Wild Rice Mix

Ingredients:

1 cup dry long-grain, brown rice

½ cup dry wild rice

1 tablespoon dried parsley

2 teaspoons all-purpose seasoning blend (I use Mrs.

Dash "Table Blend")

1 teaspoon dried thyme

Mix all of the ingredients together in a mixing bowl. Your rice mix is ready to use right away, or it can be stored in an airtight Ziploc bag for up to 3 months.

To make the rice, bring 3-1/4 cups water to a boil in a saucepan over medium heat. Add in the entire rice mix and stir to blend. Cover saucepan with a tight fitting lid, reduce heat and cook at a low simmer for 50-55 minutes. Do not open the lid during cooking time. Remove from heat, keep saucepan cover on and let the rice sit for 10 minutes. After 10 minutes, remove cover and fluff the rice up with a fork. Makes 4-5 servings.

Basil Garlic Green Beans with Pine Nuts

Ingredients:

1-1/2 pounds of fresh green beans (ends trimmed and rough chopped)

2-1/2 tablespoons olive oil

¼-1/3 cup pine nuts

3 fresh garlic cloves (minced)

12-14 fresh basil leaves (rough chopped)

Bring a large pot of salted water to a boil. Add in the chopped green beans and boil for 5 minutes. Drain and immediately plunge them into a large bowl of ice water. Drain again, and pat any excess water away with some paper towels.

Heat the olive oil in a large skillet over medium heat. Once heated, add in the pine nuts and sauté for 5 minutes while stirring frequently to prevent burning. Stir in the minced garlic and sauté for an additional 1 minutes while stirring continuously. Add in the green beans, reduce heat slightly and cook for 4-5 minutes. Stir in the chopped basil and cook for a final 1 minute. Season with sea salt and black pepper to taste and serve with an optional garnish of fresh lemon wedges. Makes 6 servings.

Garlic and Rosemary Potatoes and Onions

(preheat oven to 375 degrees and lightly oil a 8x8 inch baking dish)

Ingredients:

6 large russet potatoes (peeled and cut into thin slices)

1 large yellow onion (rough chopped)

2 sprigs fresh rosemary (rough chopped)

4 fresh garlic cloves (minced)

olive oil (to taste)

Combine the sliced potatoes, chopped onions, rosemary and garlic in a large mixing bowl and toss to evenly coat and combine all ingredients. Transfer into your baking dish and evenly drizzle olive oil across the top. Season fairly generously with sea salt and black pepper and bake on center oven rack for 30 minutes.

After 30 minutes, remove the potatoes so that you can give them a good stir. Drizzle on a little more olive oil and return to oven for another 20-30 minutes, or until potatoes are fork tender. Remove from oven and let potatoes stand for 5 minutes before serving. Makes 4-6 servings.

Herbed English Yorkshire Pudding

(batter needs to sit at room temperature for a minimum of 4-6 hours before baking – you will need a 12 count muffin tin)

Ingredients:

2 cups all-purpose flour

1 cup plain, non-dairy milk

3 large eggs

1 teaspoon Herbs de Provence seasoning blend

pinch of sea salt

Sift the flour into a mixing bowl and add in the all of the remaining ingredients. Beat at high speed until mixture forms a thick batter consistency, about 5 minutes. Cover mixing bowl with plastic wrap and let sit at room temperature for a minimum of 4-6 hours.

When ready to bake, preheat oven to 425 degrees. Oil a 12 count muffin tin and place on center oven rack to preheat along with the oven. Once oven is preheated, remove the muffin tin (the oil will be slightly smoking) and fill each compartment about 2/3 full with batter. Return to oven and bake for 20 minutes. Turn off oven and let the Yorkshire pudding "cure" in the oven for 10-20 minutes to prevent them from collapsing. Serve as-is, or with a delicious gravy poured on top.

Makes 12 Yorkshire puddings.

Garlic Kale with Caramelized Onions

Ingredients:

1 large bunch of kale (stems removed, thoroughly washed and dried and rough chopped)

1 small white or yellow onion (cut into thin, half rings)

3-4 fresh garlic cloves (minced)

1 tablespoon olive oil

balsamic vinegar (to taste)

Heat the olive oil in a saucepan over medium heat. Add in the sliced onions and cook until caramelized, about 8-10 minutes. Don't over stir the onions while cooking. Once the onions are caramelized, stir in the minced garlic and sauté until fragrant while stirring continuously, about 1 minute. Add in the hand torn kale and give it a good stir to thoroughly combine all ingredients. Cook until kale is wilted but not overly soggy. Remove from heat and drizzle in balsamic vinegar to taste. Season with sea salt and black pepper and serve. Makes 4 servings.

Traditional Southern Fried Okra

Ingredients:

1 bag (16 ounces) frozen okra (I use Pictsweet all natural okra)

1 to 2 cups cornmeal

1 to 2 cups all-purpose flour

1 teaspoon Cajun seasoning blend (or more, to taste)

5 large eggs (beaten)

Thaw the okra and thoroughly pat it dry with paper towels. Set up your assembly line: Place the thawed, dried okra in a bowl. Next, place your beaten eggs in a bowl. Whisk together the cornmeal, flour and Cajun seasoning in a bowl and place it next to the bowl with the beaten eggs.

Preheat a thin layer of oil in a large skillet or wok over medium-high heat. Dredge the okra pieces first through the egg mixture and then roll them through the breading mixture until evenly coated. Once oil is heated, arrange the okra in a single layer (be careful to not overcrowd the skillet) and fry until golden brown, stirring and turning during cooking to ensure even cooking and browning. Drain the fried okra on a paper towel lined plate and serve. I like to serve these over a bed of freshly steamed rice and beans for a delicious Southern style vegetarian meal. Makes 4 servings.

Sesame Broccoli

Ingredients:

1 large bunch of broccoli (cut into florets, leaving a little bit of stem on each)

1 tablespoon toasted sesame oil

2 tablespoons toasted sesame seeds

4 ounces – 8 ounces sliced water chestnuts (optional)

1 tablespoon Braggs liquid aminos (may substitute with Tamari or regular soy sauce)

Bring a large pot of salted water to a boil. Add in the prepped broccoli and cook until broccoli is BARELY fork tender. Drain and use paper towels to pat away excess water. Heat the sesame oil in a large skillet or wok over medium-high heat. Once heated, add in the sesame seeds, water chestnuts (if using) and cooked broccoli. Stir fry until both the water chestnuts and broccoli are thoroughly heated through. Turn off heat and drizzle in the liquid aminos (or Tamari or soy sauce) and give everything a good toss to evenly coat and blend before serving. Makes 4-6 servings.

Broiled Cheesy Zucchini Rounds

(preheat oven to broil – you need an un-greased 9x13 inch baking dish)

Ingredients:

6 large sized zucchini (peeled and cut into ¼ inch thick rounds)

2-1/2 cups vegetable broth

3-4 fresh garlic cloves (minced)

1 cup shredded Sharp Cheddar cheese

½ cup freshly grated or shaved Parmesan cheese

Bring the vegetable broth to a boil in a saucepan over medium heat. Add in the zucchini rounds and cook until zucchini is BARELY fork tender. Drain and pat dry any excess water with some paper towels. Evenly arrange half of the cooked zucchini in your baking dish. Sprinkle the minced garlic evenly across the top, followed by half of the shredded Sharp Cheddar cheese and half of the Parmesan cheese. Repeat another layer with the remaining zucchini, Sharp Cheddar cheese and Parmesan cheese. Broil until cheese becomes bubbly and melts, about 2 minutes. Remove from oven, season with sea salt and black pepper to taste and serve. Makes 4-6 servings. *If your zucchini are on the small side, use an 8x8 inch baking dish instead and decrease the amount of vegetable broth to 2 cups.

Easy Potato Pancakes

Ingredients:

2-3 cups finely grated potatoes (I recommend Russet)

2 tablespoons finely minced yellow onion

2 large eggs (well beaten)

2 tablespoons all-purpose flour

1-2 fresh garlic cloves (minced – omit if you prefer a sweeter potato pancake)

Whisk together the eggs and flour in a large mixing bowl until well blended. Add in all of the remaining ingredients and stir and work mixture with your hands until everything comes together. Season the potato mixture with sea salt and black pepper to taste and give mixture another stir to blend. Heat a thin layer of olive oil in a large skillet over medium-high heat. Shape the potato mixture into small, thin rounds (think 'dollar pancakes'). Once the oil is heated, place several of the potato pancakes in the skillet (do not overcrowd) and cook for about 3 minutes on each side, until golden brown and crispy. Transfer the potato pancakes to a paper towel-lined plate to drain any excess oil. Cover plate with a clean towel to keep warm while you finish cooking the remaining pancakes. Makes 4 servings. *Serves well as-is, or with a drizzle of gravy for even more savory flavor, or with a generous spoonful of applesauce for a nice sweet and savory flavor combination.

Sweet and Tangy Roasted Carrots

(preheat oven to 375 degrees – you need an ungreased 8x8 inch baking dish)

Ingredients:

1 pound bag of baby carrots (cut in half lengthwise)

2 tablespoons olive oil

2 tablespoons brown sugar

1 tablespoon balsamic vinegar

Bring a pot of salted water to a boil. Drop in the halved baby carrots and cook just until carrots are fork tender but still have some crisp to them. Drain and thoroughly pat dry any excess water with paper towels. Arrange the carrots in your un-greased baking dish. Evenly drizzle the olive oil, brown sugar and balsamic vinegar across the top. Season with sea salt and black pepper to taste and roast on center oven rack for 30 minutes. Remove from oven and let sit for a few minutes before serving. Makes 4 servings.

CHAPTER 5 – ENTREES

Gina 'The Veggie Goddess' Matthews

Baked Stuffed Portobello Caps

(preheat oven to 450 degrees and very lightly grease a cookie sheet or large shallow baking dish)

Ingredients:

4 large Portobello mushroom caps (inner grills carefully removed)

¼ cup fine breadcrumbs (plain or seasoned)

2 tablespoons freshly grated Parmesan cheese (may also use prepared Parmesan)

1 tablespoon finely chopped fresh parsley

1-2 tablespoons olive oil

Place the mushroom caps (grill side up) on your prepared cookie sheet, sprinkle with a little sea salt and roast on center oven rack until tender, about 20-25 minutes.

While mushrooms are roasting, combine the breadcrumbs, Parmesan cheese, chopped parsley and olive oil in a small mixing bowl and whisk until all the ingredients are well combined. Add in sea salt and black pepper to taste and stir to blend. Once the mushrooms are tender, remove from oven and evenly spoon some of the filling mixture into each of the mushroom caps, about 2 tablespoons for each. Return to oven and roast until the breadcrumb mixture becomes golden brown, about 5-7 minutes. Remove from oven and serve with your favorite side dish or salad. Makes 4 servings.

Grilled Mediterranean Pizza

(preheat outdoor or indoor grill to medium-high)

Ingredients:

1 pound prepared pizza dough (divided into 4 even pieces of dough)

½ cup prepared pesto sauce

4 ripe Roma tomatoes (thinly sliced)

½ cup finely crumbled Feta cheese

¼ cup rough chopped fresh basil leaves

While your grill is preheating, on a well floured surface roll out each of the 4 dough sections into a rough 8 inch sized circle. ((f you prefer, you can alternately roll each dough section into a square shape.) Each rolled out section of pizza dough should be about ¼ inch thick. Once your grill is preheated, lay the crusts on the grill and cook until they are lightly puffed and the bottoms of the crust are a light golden brown, about 3-4 minutes.

Flip over the crusts and immediately evenly spread the pesto sauce onto each crust. Next, top each crust evenly with the sliced tomatoes, crumbled Feta cheese and chopped basil. Close grill lid (or cover loosely with aluminum foil) and grill for an additional 3-5 minutes. Remove from grill and let sit for 3 minutes before serving. Makes 4 servings.

Classic Spaghetti Genovese

Ingredients:

8 ounces spaghetti (regular, whole wheat or gluten free)

2 heaping cups baby spinach

1 cup thinly sliced OR diced baby red potatoes

1 pound fresh green beans (ends trimmed and cut into 1 inch pieces)

½ cup prepared pesto sauce

*You will be using the same large saucepot to make this dish.

Bring a large pot of salted water to a boil. Drop in the baby spinach and cook for 30-45 SECONDS, just until wilted. Using a slotted spoon, transfer wilted spinach into a blender. Keep the pot of water boiling and add in the spaghetti and sliced (or diced) potatoes. Cook until barely tender, about 5-6 minutes and then drop in the cut green beans. Continue cooking for another 3-4 minutes. Just before the spaghetti is done cooking, ladle out 1 cup of the cooking liquid. Pour HALF of the liquid (1/2 cup) into the blender with the wilted spinach, and add in the pesto sauce along with sea salt and black pepper to taste. Puree until smooth, stopping to scrape down the sides as necessary. *Keep the other ½ cup of cooking liquid to the side.

Drain the spaghetti, potatoes and green beans and immediately return them to the empty saucepan. Add in the pesto sauce, stir to evenly coat all ingredients and heat over medium heat until everything is heated through and well combined, about 2 minutes. If the sauce is too thick, you can drizzle in some of the reserved cooking liquid to reach desired consistency. Makes 4 servings.

Spinach Quiche Cups

(preheat oven to 400 degrees and lightly oil 8 large muffin tin compartments)

Ingredients:

12 ounces fresh baby spinach

½ cup ricotta cheese

½ cup freshly grated Parmesan cheese (may also use prepared Parmesan cheese)

2 large eggs OR 3 medium eggs (well beaten)

1-2 cloves fresh garlic (minced)

Finely chop all of the baby spinach OR you can toss it into a food processor and pulse a few times until spinach is rough chopped. Put the chopped spinach into a large mixing bowl. Add in all of the remaining ingredients along with sea salt and black pepper to taste and stir until all ingredients are well combined. Evenly divide mixture into the 8 oiled muffin tin compartments. They should be filled to the top. Bake on center oven rack for 20-25 minutes. Remove from oven and let the quiche rest in the muffin tin pan for 5 minutes before carefully loosening the edges with a knife and removing from pan. Makes a great brunch or anytime special meal and serves well with a side of fresh fruit or raw julienne veggies. Makes 4 servings of 2 quiche cups each.

Garlic Quinoa Stuffed Bell Peppers

(preheat oven to 350 degrees and fill a 8x8 inch baking dish with about ¼ inch water)

Ingredients:

4 extra large bell peppers (red, orange, yellow or green)

1-1/2 cups cooked quinoa

6 fresh garlic cloves (minced)

1-1/2 cups cooked vegetable add-in of your choice, rough chopped (mushrooms, asparagus, eggplant, green beans, corn, more bell peppers, etc.)

olive oil

*This is a great way to whip up a fast and healthy dinner using leftover cooked quinoa and leftover cooked veggies.

Slice off the top of each bell pepper, and carefully hollow out the insides by scraping with a spoon.

Combine the cooked quinoa, minced garlic and chopped cooked vegetables of your choice into a large mixing bowl. Drizzle in enough olive to lightly moisten ingredients along with sea salt and black pepper to taste. Stir until everything is well combined. Evenly stuff the quinoa mixture into each hollowed out bell pepper and place into your water-filled baking dish. Bake on center oven rack for 25-35 minutes, until the peppers are tender and the quinoa filling is thoroughly heated through. Makes 4 servings. *You can alternately stuff some carved out zucchini halves with the quinoa filling and bake for the same amount of time. Just cut 6-8 large zucchini in half lengthwise, and using a small spoon scrape out a deep groove down the middle of each half.

Rice and Bean Burritos

(preheat oven to 375 degrees)

Ingredients:

1 can (15 ounce) black beans (with the liquid)

1-1/2 cups cooked rice (any kind)

½-3/4 teaspoon of chili seasoning powder (*try the one listed in the bonus seasoning blends chapter)

8 large burrito sized flour tortillas

¾ cup shredded Pepper Jack cheese (or any other cheese your prefer)

While the oven is preheating, combine the black beans (with their liquid), cooked rice and chili seasoning powder in a saucepan over medium heat. Stir frequently until mixture is evenly heated through, about 5 minutes. Evenly spoon the rice and beans mixture into the center of each of the 8 tortillas. Next, evenly top each with the shredded cheese and roll them up. Place the prepared burritos seam side down onto an ungreased cookie sheet and bake on center oven rack for 8-10 minutes. Remove from oven and serve as-is, or with your favorite burrito extras (salsa, sour cream, fresh chopped cilantro, fresh lime wedges, etc.) Makes 4-8 servings.

South-of-the-Border Stuffed Poblano Peppers

(preheat oven to 400 degrees)

Ingredients:

4 large poblano peppers (halved lengthwise and seeded)

1 can (15 ounce) refried beans

1 cup cooked rice (a great way to use leftover rice)

½ cup picante sauce

6 ounces shredded cheese (Mexican cheese blend, Pepper Jack or Colby are the best choices)

Arrange the 8 poblano pepper halves in a single layer on a cookie sheet, cut side up. Roast for 15 minutes. While peppers are roasting, combine the refried beans, cooked rice and picante sauce in a mixing bowl. Stir until all ingredients are well combined.

Once the peppers are done roasting remove from oven and allow them to cool enough to handle. Evenly fill each pepper half with the rice-bean mixture. Next, evenly sprinkle the cheese on top of each one. Return to oven and bake for 10-12 minutes. Serve as-is, or with your favorite toppings such as sour cream, fresh chopped cilantro and fresh lime wedges. Makes 4 servings of 2 stuffed pepper halves each.

Baked Cheesy Ziti

(preheat oven to 350 degrees and lightly oil bottom and sides of 9x13 inch baking dish)

Ingredients:

8 ounces dry ziti pasta

1 container (16 ounce) ricotta cheese

3 cups shredded Mozzarella cheese (divided)

½ cup freshly grated Parmesan cheese (fresh vs. container Parmesan is highly preferred)

3 cups marinara sauce (divided)

Bring a large pot of salted water to a boil. Add in the ziti pasta and cook to al dente' according to package directions. Drain, rinse and drain again.

In a large mixing bowl, stir together the container of ricotta cheese along with half (1-1/2 cups) of the shredded Mozzarella cheese. Add in the cooked ziti pasta and toss to evenly coat and blend. Pour half (1-1/2 cups) of the marinara sauce into prepared baking dish and evenly spoon the ziti mixture on top. Pour the remaining marinara sauce on top of the ziti mixture. Evenly sprinkle the freshly grated Parmesan cheese on top of the marinara layer, followed by the remaining 1-1/2 cups of Mozzarella cheese. Bake on center oven rack for 25-30 minutes, until top is bubbly and golden brown. Remove from oven and let the ziti sit for 5-7 minutes before serving. Makes 6-8 servings.

Peasant Style Mock Kielbasa and Cabbage Stew

Ingredients:

2 packages (14 ounces each) of Tofurky vegetarian Kielbasa (cut into 1 inch pieces)

1 large head of green cabbage (chopped and core discarded)

6 large potatoes (peeled and cut into big chunk sized pieces)

1 large yellow onion (rough diced)

4-5 fresh garlic cloves (minced)

Combine all of the prepped ingredients in a large saucepot and cover with enough water so that it covers all but the top 2 inches or so. Bring to a boil over medium-high heat, immediately reduce heat and cook at a low simmer until all of the cabbage is cooked down and the potatoes are fork tender, about 15-20 minutes. Give the stew a good stir twice during cooking time. Remove from heat, drain any excess water and season with sea salt and black pepper to taste. Stew serves well with a basket of warm, crusty bread. Makes 6-8 servings.

Tex Mex Casserole

(preheat oven to 350 degrees and lightly oil bottom of 9x13 inch baking dish)

Ingredients:

1 bag (12 ounces) Morningstar Farms Meal Starter Crumbles (this is a ground hamburger substitute)

1 package (16 ounce) penne pasta

32 ounces of your favorite salsa (I recommend a medium heat to high heat level)

1 can (15 ounces) black beans (rinsed and drained)

2 heaping cups shredded Mexican cheese blend (divided)

Cook the pasta in a large pot of salted water to al dente' according to package directions. Drain, rinse and drain again. Thaw the meal starter crumbles at room temperature while pasta is cooking.

In a large mixing bowl, combine the cooked pasta, meal starter crumbles, salsa and black beans, and stir to evenly combine all ingredients. Spread half of the mixture into your oiled baking dish and cover with half of the shredded cheese. Repeat with the remaining casserole base mixture, followed by the remaining shredded cheese. Bake on center oven rack for 40-45 minutes. Remove from oven and let the casserole stand for 5-7 minutes before serving. Makes 4-6 servings.

Mock Chicken Teriyaki Stir Fry

Ingredients:

4 vegetarian chicken filets (I use Gardein brand – Chick'n Scallopini filets)

2 teaspoons sesame oil

1 cup of your favorite teriyaki sauce

3 fresh garlic cloves (minced)

¼ cup freshly squeezed lemon juice

Thaw the vegetarian chicken filets just enough to be able to safely cut up into diced sized pieces. Heat the sesame oil in a wok or large skillet, over medium-high heat. Once hot, add in the diced vegetarian chicken pieces and sauté while stirring frequently for 4-5 minutes. Add in the teriyaki sauce, minced garlic and lemon juice and continue sautéing while stirring frequently for another 4-5 minutes, or until all ingredients are thoroughly heated through. Turn off heat and let the stir fry rest in the pan for several minutes. Serve as-is or over a bed of buckwheat noodles or freshly steamed rice. Makes 4 servings.

Spinach and Cheese Stuffed Acorn Squash Bowls

(preheat oven to 400 degrees)

Ingredients:

2 acorn squash (each cut in half and inner seeds and strings removed)

1 package (10 ounces) frozen spinach (thawed and squeezed thoroughly dry)

1-1/2 cups of shredded gruyere cheese (divided)

1/3 cup finely chopped nuts (walnuts or pecans)

4 fresh garlic cloves (minced)

Arrange the prepped acorn squash halves (save the seeds for roasting) on a cookie sheet, cut side down, and roast in preheated oven on center oven rack for 25-30 minutes until liquid oozes out when flesh is pierced with a fork.

While the squash is roasting, combine the thawed, dried spinach in a mixing bowl with 1 cup of the shredded cheese, the chopped nuts, minced garlic and lots of sea salt and black pepper to taste. Stir to evenly coat and blend all ingredients. After the squash has roasted for 30 minutes, remove from oven and turn them over so that the cut side is facing up. Evenly fill each squash half with the spinach mixture and then top with the remaining ½ cup of shredded cheese. Return to oven and roast for an additional 20-25 minutes. Remove from oven and let stand for 5-7 minutes before serving. Makes 4 servings.

Spaghetti Squash "Pasta" with Garlic Butter Parmesan Sauce

(preheat oven to 375 degrees)

Ingredients:

1 large spaghetti squash

½ cup freshly grated Parmesan cheese

¼ cup of butter (salted)

1-2 fresh garlic cloves (minced)

1 tablespoon freshly chopped basil

Using a sharp knife, poke holes on all sides of the squash. Place in a baking dish and roast in preheated oven until tender, about 45-60 minutes. *Because the size and density of the squash will vary, I recommend removing the squash at the 45 minute mark. Cut it in half lengthwise. If you can easily pierce the inner flesh, it is ready. If it is a bit on the hard side still, return to oven and bake until flesh is soft but not mushy.

Once squash is roasted to correct doneness, scoop out the inner seeds and strings and discard. Using a fork, rake it across the flesh to loosen and extract all the "spaghetti" like strands. Put all of the spaghetti squash strands into a large mixing bowl along with the grated Parmesan cheese and ¼ cup of butter and the minced garlic, and toss to evenly coat and blend. Season squash with sea salt and black pepper to taste. If you desire more butter, add it in now. Stir in the freshly chopped basil and give the squash a final toss to blend before serving. Makes 2 servings.

Slow Cooker Indian Rice and Lentils

(you need a crock pot for this recipe)

Ingredients:

1 cup basmati rice

1 tablespoon garam masla Indian spice blend

3-1/2 cups vegetable broth

½ cup lentils (any will work, but I make this with green lentils)

3 fresh garlic cloves (minced)

Combine all of the ingredients in a crock pot and give it a good stir to blend. Set crock pot on "high" and allow mixture to come to a boil. Immediately reduce cook setting to "low" and cook for 5 hours or until both rice and lentils are fully cooked. If you are setting this before leaving for work or school and can't wait for mixture to come to a simmer before reducing heat, then set the crock pot to "low" and cook for 6 to 6-1/2 hours. Serve with some warm pita bread for a hearty healthy meal. Makes 4 servings. *If you like and tolerate spicier flavors, you can add in some hot curry powder to taste and heat preference.

Greek Brunch Frittatas

(position oven rack to the top 1/3 of the oven and preheat oven to broil – you will need a cast iron skillet or other ovenproof skillet)

Ingredients:

8 large eggs

2 heaping tablespoons of freshly chopped oregano

2 tablespoons olive oil

1 cup diced red bell pepper

½ cup finely crumbled Feta cheese

In a mixing bowl, whisk together the eggs until well beaten. Stir in the freshly chopped oregano along with a generous pinch of sea salt and black pepper. Heat the olive oil in a cast iron skillet over medium heat. Once heated, add in the diced bell peppers and sauté for 2-3 minutes. Carefully pour the egg mixture on top of the sautéed bell peppers. Cook for 3-4 minutes, and gently lift up around the edges using a spatula. Turn off heat and evenly sprinkle the finely crumbled Feta cheese on top of the eggs.

Transfer the skillet into your preheated oven and broil until the top is a nice golden brown, about 2-4 minutes. Remove from oven and let the frittata rest in the skillet for several minutes before cutting into pie shaped slices and serving. Makes 4 servings. *I like to serve this with a generous garnish of finely diced green onion.

Gina 'The Veggie Goddess' Matthews

CHAPTER 6 – DESSERTS

Gina 'The Veggie Goddess' Matthews

Baked Peaches and Granola

(preheat oven to 350 degrees - add 2 tablespoons of water into bottom of 9x13 inch baking dish)

Ingredients:

4 ripe, large peaches (make sure they are not too soft)

6 tablespoons butter (DIVIDED - regular or vegan – softened to room temperature)

2/3 cup sweet granola mix (one that has dried fruit)

ground cinnamon to garnish (optional)

Carefully cut each of the peaches in half and remove the pit. Place all 8 peach halves into your baking dish with the 2 tablespoons of water, cut side up, and place 1 teaspoon (NOT tablespoon) of the butter into each of the peach halves. (roughly half of the called for amount of butter) Bake on center oven rack for 25-30 minutes, until peaches are tender and very lightly browned. Remove from oven and set aside.

While the peaches are cooling slightly, melt the remaining butter in a skillet or saucepan over medium heat. Once melted, add in the sweet granola mix and stir until the granola is evenly coated with the melted butter. Arrange the baked peach halves onto a single large serving platter or 4 individual serving dishes, and top with the buttered-granola mixture. Serve with an optional sprinkle of ground cinnamon. Makes 4 servings of 2 baked peach halves each.

Easy Chocolate Mousse

Ingredients:

7 ounces semi-sweet chocolate chips

2 large egg yolks

2 tablespoons raw sugar

1-1/4 cups heavy cream (divided)

Combine the egg yolks and raw sugar in a small mixing bowl and whisk until mixture is well blended and pale golden in color.

Pour ¼ cup of the heavy cream into a saucepan and bring to a very low simmer over low heat. Do not attempt to rush the process by heating over higher heat. It won't take but a few minutes. Once the cream has been brought to a low simmer, SLOWLY pour it into the bowl with the egg yolk-sugar mixture while stirring to blend. Immediately pour the cream mixture back into the saucepan and simmer over low heat for 2-3 minutes, until mixture lightly coats the back of a wooden spoon or silicone spatula.

Put the chocolate chips into a heat proof bowl and SLOWLY pour in the hot cream mixture while stirring continuously until all of the chocolate is fully melted and everything is well blended and creamy smooth.

Using an electric mixer beat the remaining 1 cup of heavy cream until stiff peaks form. Gently fold in the whipped cream, half at a time, into the chocolate mixture just until all ingredients are fully incorporated. Spoon the mixture into one large serving bowl or 4 small individual serving cups, cover with plastic wrap and chill in the fridge for a minimum of 2-3 hours before serving. Makes 4 servings. You can serve with an optional garnish of fresh fruit, fresh chopped nuts, fresh whipped cream or a dusting of powdered sugar.

Pecan Meringue Cookies

(preheat oven to 225 degrees and line 2 large cookie sheets with parchment paper)

Ingredients:

4 large egg whites (at room temperature)

¼ teaspoon pure vanilla extract

¼ teaspoon cream of tartar

1 cup of raw sugar

½ cup of finely crushed pecans

Combine the room temperature egg whites, vanilla extract and cream of tartar in a mixing bowl and using an electric mixer beat at high speed until soft peaks form. Continue to beat on high while slowly adding in the 1 cup of raw sugar, a little at a time, along with a pinch of sea salt until stiff peaks form, about 3-4 minutes. Gently fold in the finely crushed pecans.

Drop the mixture by spoonfuls onto your parchment lined cookie sheets about 1-1/2 inches apart. Bake the meringue cookies for 2 to 2-1/2 hours, until they are dried. Rotate cookie sheets midway through cooking time. Remove from oven and allow the cookies to rest on the cookie sheet for 15-30 minutes before removing. Store any leftover cookies at room temperature in a tightly sealed container. Makes approximately 2 dozen cookies.

Frozen Lemon Cups

(you will need a 6 jumbo sized muffin cup tin OR a regular sized 12 count muffin tin)

Ingredients:

½ cup raw sugar

6 large egg yolks (at room temperature)

zest from 3 large lemons

½ cup of fresh squeezed lemon juice

2 cups of heavy cream

Combine the raw sugar and room temperature egg yolks in a mixing bowl and whisk until well combined. Add in the lemon zest and lemon juice and stir until mixture is well blended. Transfer mixture into a saucepan and cook over medium-low heat until mixture resembles the consistency of gravy, about 8 minutes. *Be sure to stir almost continuously for proper consistency. Spoon mixture into a glass or ceramic bowl and allow it to cool to room temperature. Once it has reached room temperature, cover with plastic wrap, being sure to place directly on top of the lemony curd mixture to prevent a "skin" from forming. Place bowl in the fridge to allow mixture to firm.

Once the lemon curd mixture has firmed, remove from the fridge and take off the plastic wrap. Using a large fork or a whisk, gently stir the lemon curd mixture. Next, beat the 2 cups of heavy cream in a chilled bowl using an electric mixer on high speed until stiff peaks form. Gently fold in the whipped cream into the lemon curd mixture just until blended and no white shows. Evenly spoon the mixture into your 6 jumbo muffin cup tin or 10-12 regular muffin cup tin, and smooth the tops with the back of a water moistened spoon. Cover with plastic wrap and place the muffin tray onto a small cookie sheet. Place in freezer and freeze for a minimum of 4-5 hours before serving. To serve, remove from freezer and let stand at room temperature for 8-10 minutes. Carefully remove (or invert) your frozen lemon treats onto one large serving platter, or onto individual serving plates. Serve as-is or with a topping of fresh fruit, chocolate syrup or both. Makes 6 servings.

Vanilla Shortbread Cookies

(preheat oven to 350 degrees and line a large cookie sheet with parchment paper)

Ingredients:

1-1/2 cups all-purpose flour

2 sticks of butter (salted - at room temperature)

½ cup powdered sugar

½ teaspoon pure vanilla extract

Combine all ingredients in a mixing bowl and beat on high speed for a FULL 10 minutes. *You can use a stand mixer or a hand-held electric mixer, but make sure you beat at high speed and for the full 10 minutes. Mixture will be mealy at first, but it will come together during the final couple minutes of beating. Once the batter is ready, drop by teaspoon sized amounts onto your parchment-lined cookie sheet and bake on center oven rack for 10-15 minutes until the bottoms are a light golden brown. You do not want the tops to become golden brown however, so keep a close watch on them starting at the 10 minute cooking mark. Remove cookies from oven and let them sit for 5 minutes on cookie sheet before transferring them to a wire rack to fully cool. Makes 24-30 cookies, depending on size.

Italian Balsamic Strawberries

Ingredients:

1 pint firm, ripe strawberries (hulled and cut into quarters lengthwise)

2 tablespoons raw sugar

1-1/2 tablespoons balsamic vinegar (do NOT substitute with any other kind of strawberries)

In a large mixing bowl, whisk together the raw sugar and balsamic vinegar. Add in the cut strawberry pieces and toss until evenly coated. Let the strawberries sit at room temperature until they start to "juice" (the sugar-vinegar mixture will extract the natural juices) and then cover and move the strawberries to the fridge to chill for 1 hour before serving. Makes 4 servings.

*This is not a make the night before kind of dessert. You ideally want to make and serve this delicious dessert within 1-2 hours after chilling in the fridge, otherwise the strawberries will start to get soggy.

Warm Banana Coconut Dessert Soup

Ingredients:

4 large bananas (you want them firm and just a tad under-ripe)

2 cups coconut milk (the kind you get in a can)

4 tablespoons raw sugar (or more to taste)

½ teaspoon ground cinnamon

Peel the bananas and cut them into bite sized rounds, and then set them aside. Bring the coconut milk to a low boil in a saucepan over medium heat. Add in the raw sugar and cinnamon and stir continuously until both are fully dissolved. Stir in the bananas, reduce heat and simmer for 2-4 minutes until bananas are tender but not mushy. Ladle into individual soup or dessert bowls and serve as-is or with an optional added garnish: sprinkle of cinnamon, dollop of fresh whipped cream, a sprinkle of finely shredded coconut. Makes 4 servings.

Mini Pecan Pie Cupcakes

(preheat oven to 350 degrees and lightly oil 2 – 12 count mini cupcake tins)

Ingredients:

½ cup all-purpose flour

1 cup packed brown sugar

2 large eggs (at room temperature)

2/3 cup melted butter (salted)

1 cup finely chopped pecans

Sift the flour into a mixing bowl and in the brown sugar, eggs and melted butter. Stir by hand until all ingredients are moistened and thoroughly and evenly blended. Fold in the finely chopped pecans and then spoon the batter into the oiled mini cupcake tins, filling each one ¾ of the way full. Bake on center oven rack for 15-20 minutes. Remove from oven and let the cupcakes cool for 20-30 minutes in the tins before removing and transferring to a wire rack to finish cooling. Makes 24 mini cupcakes.

Nutty Chocolate Orange Fudge

(line bottom and sides of an 8x8 inch baking dish with waxed paper and then lightly oil)

Ingredients:

2-1/2 cups chocolate chips (semi-sweet)

1 can (14 ounce) condensed milk (sweetened)

½ cup finely chopped nuts (pecans, walnuts or macadamia)

2 teaspoons fresh orange zest

Combine the chocolate chips and condensed milk in a saucepan over medium-low heat, and cook while stirring continuously until chocolate is fully melted. *Do NOT try to rush the process by cooking over high heat. Once the chocolate is melted, remove saucepan from heat and stir in the chopped nuts and orange zest. Spread the mixture into your prepared dish, cover with plastic wrap or foil and chill in the fridge until set. When fudge is set, carefully remove it by the corners of the waxed paper or foil and set onto a cutting board. Cut the fudge into desired sized pieces and store in a tightly sealed container in the fridge until ready to serve. Makes about 12-24 pieces of cut fudge, depending on size.

Tofu Banana Split Dessert Salad

Ingredients:

6 small, ripe bananas (peeled and cut into half lengthwise)

1-1/2 pints firm or extra-firm tofu (crumbled)

1-1/4 cups any variety of small berries (blueberries, raspberries, etc.)

¼ cup diced strawberries

¼ cup finely chopped nuts (walnuts, pecans, etc.)

Arrange 2 sliced banana halves onto 6 individual serving plates or bowls. Evenly top each with the crumbled tofu, berries, diced strawberries and chopped nuts. Serve as is or with an optional added topping: fresh whipped cream, dried fruit or a drizzle melted caramel or chocolate sauce. Makes 6 servings.

Italian Wedding Cookies

(preheat oven to 350 degrees and line a large cookie sheet with parchment paper)

Ingredients:

2 cups all-purpose flour

1 cup powdered sugar (plus extra for dusting)

2 sticks of butter (salted – softened to room temperature)

1 teaspoon pure vanilla extract

1 cup very finely chopped pecans

Sift the flour and powdered sugar into a large mixing bowl. Add in the softened butter and vanilla extract and beat on medium-low speed to first blend and then at medium-high speed until mixture becomes creamy and well blended. Stir in the finely chopped pecans by hand until just evenly blended. Shape the batter into very tightly packed 1-1/2 inch sized balls. Arrange in a single layer on your parchment lined cookie sheet and bake on center oven rack for 10-15 minutes, until BARELY golden brown. Remove from oven and leave the cookies on the cookie sheet. Immediately dust the tops with some more powdered sugar and then let the cookies fully cool on the cookie sheet before transferring to a serving platter. Makes approximately 30-36 cookies.

White Chocolate Lemon Bark

(line a cookie sheet with waxed paper or parchment paper)

Ingredients:

2 bags (12 ounces each) good quality white chocolate chips

1 cup finely crushed lemon drop candies

SLOWLY melt the chocolate chips in a saucepan over medium-low heat while stirring continuously. Once melted, remove from heat and stir in the crushed lemon drop candies. Carefully spread the mixture into a ¼ inch thick square (or any other shape you'd like) onto your waxed paper lined cookie sheet. Transfer cookie sheet to the fridge to allow the bark to set. Once the bark is fully chilled and set, break off into pieces and serve. Store any leftover bark in a tightly sealed container in the fridge. Makes about 8 servings.

Design Your Own Dessert Crepes

(you will need a 6 inch skillet)

Ingredients:

1 cup all-purpose flour

1-1/2 cups plain, non-dairy milk

2 large eggs (at room temperature - beaten)

1 teaspoon light oil (safflower, sunflower, grapeseed, etc.) + more for cooking

¼ teaspoon sea salt

Sift the flour into a mixing bowl. Stir in the milk, beaten eggs, oil and sea salt and stir until all ingredients are moistened and well combined. Heat a lightly oiled 6 inch skillet over medium heat. Once heated, remove from heat and drop in 2 tablespoons of the batter into the middle of the skillet and tilt from side-to-side until the batter evenly coats the bottom of the skillet. Return skillet to heat and cook until crepe is browned on the bottom side only, 1-2 minutes. To remove, flip the skillet over onto a paper towel lined plate and repeat process with the remaining crepe batter. Once all of the crepes have been prepared, simply fill with your favorite dessert fillings and toppings (ie: fresh fruit and whipped cream; custard and chocolate syrup; fruit and nuts; mousse and powdered sugar, etc.) and serve. Makes 6-7 crepes.

Warm Cinnamon Dusted Orange and Apple Rings

Ingredients:

2 large sweet oranges (the sweeter the better – bland tasting oranges will not hold up to this recipe)

2 large sweet apples (again, the sweeter the better)

1-2 tablespoons ground cinnamon

Peel both the oranges and apples and cut into thin sliced rings. Remove seeds. Heat a grill, griddle or skillet to medium heat. (do not add any oil) Once preheated, arrange the orange and apple slices in a single layer, being careful to not overcrowd, and heat for 1 minute on each side. Arrange the warmed fruit slices onto 4 individual serving plates in a fanned out circle, and then evenly dust with the ground cinnamon to taste. Serve as-is, or with some raisins and/or finely crushed pecans added as an optional garnish. Makes 4 servings.

Crock Pot Turtles

(you need a large sized crock pot)

Ingredients:

16 ounces (1 pound) of chopped nut pieces (pecans, walnuts, peanuts, etc.)

16 ounces (1 pound) of chopped nut pieces of a

different variety (pecans, walnuts, peanuts, etc.)

1 bag (11.5 ounces) semi-sweet chocolate chips

4 ounces dark German chocolate (broken up into pieces)

32 ounces of white almond bark (this comes in various sizes depending on brand – the one I use is in a 24 ounce package, so I use slightly less than 1-1/2 packages)

Evenly spread out the 2 pounds of chopped nut pieces into the bottom of your crock pot. Evenly arrange the chocolate chips, broken up pieces of German chocolate and almond bark (also broken up into pieces) on top of the layer of nuts. Cook on "low" for 1-3/4 hours. Line 1-2 cookie sheets with waxed paper or parchment paper. Using a spoon or melon ball scoop, scoop out the warm turtle mixture and arrange in a single layer onto your paper-lined cookie sheets. Once you have finished, let them set at room temperature before serving. Keep any leftovers in a tightly sealed container in the fridge. This recipe makes a large batch, so if you only have a medium sized crock pot just cut the recipe ingredient amounts in half. If you just have a baby sized crock pot, cut the recipe ingredients amounts into one quarter or less.

Light and Fluffy Italian Sponge Cake

(preheat oven to 350 degrees and line two 9 inch bundt pans with waxed or parchment paper)

Ingredients:

6 large eggs (yolks and whites separated)

1 cup of raw sugar (divided)

1 cup cake flour (sifted)

Combine the egg whites with ½ cup of the raw sugar in a mixing bowl, and beat on high speed until mixture forms very stiff peaks. Combine the egg yolks with the other ½ cup of raw sugar in another mixing bowl, and beat on high speed until mixture becomes very thick and is light yellow in color.

Gently fold the egg yolk mixture into the bowl with the egg white mixture, and keep gently folding until mixture is uniform in color. Next, fold in the cake flour ¼ of a cup at a time, until all ingredients are combined, but be careful to not over-mix. Evenly spoon half of the batter into each of the parchment lined bundt pans and bake them both on center oven rack for 30-35 minutes, or until toothpick comes out clean from center. Remove from oven and let the 2 halves rest for 5 minutes in the pan before removing them from the pans, and discarding the parchment paper. Let both of the cake halves cool fully. Once cooled, you can serve as-is, or fill the top of one of the cake halves with desired filling ingredients (preserves, custard, mousse, whipped cream, lemon curd, fresh berries, etc.) and then assembling the cake halves on top of each other. Makes 8-16 servings, depending on how served.

No-Bake Nut Butter Cookie Balls

(line a large cookie sheet with parchment paper)

Ingredients:

1 cup nut butter (smooth variety – almond, cashew, peanut, etc.)

1 cup raw honey (slightly warmed)

1 to 2 cups toasted wheat germ

¾ cup finely shredded coconut (or more, as needed)

Combine the nut butter and raw honey in a mixing bowl, and using a wooden spoon stir until well combined. Add in the toasted wheat germ. Start with 1 cup, and if the mixture is too stiff then gradually add in more until desired consistency is reached. You want mixture to be thick and able to hold its shape, but not so thick that you can't stir and work with it. Once mixture is to desired consistency, shape the batter into small balls with your hands. Place the shredded coconut onto a flat plate or shallow bowl and roll each cookie ball through the coconut. Arrange the cookie balls in a single layer onto your parchment-lined cookie sheet, and keep refrigerated until ready to serve.

Makes approximately 28-32 cookie balls

BONUS CHAPTER 1:
15 DIY SEASONING BLEND RECIPES

Gina 'The Veggie Goddess' Matthews

One of my aims in cooking is to always keep things as simple as possible. Whether cooking for just myself or a crowd, simplicity and shortcut preparations help make cooking an enjoyable experience even for novice cooks. In this bonus chapter, I've created 15 homemade seasoning spice blends for you to make and keep in your spice rack or pantry so you'll always have the most flavorful of spice blends readily on hand to liven up every dish you make.

I typically buy my herbs and spices in bulk, and some in larger quantities than others. You ideally only want to buy in a quantity that you will use within 6 months. Additionally, I can't recommend enough that you only purchase organic herbs and spices, and preferably from your country of origin. Often, non-organic spices have been adulterated with other ingredients that may, or may not, be listed on the label. And, most people don't know that food products are radiated once they reach customs from other countries. Radiating food completely destroys all of the health benefits of the spices, as well as greatly diminishes their freshness, aroma and taste. Quality truly matters here, so I don't optimally recommend purchasing a 25 pound sack of herbs or spices off of eBay, or from a different country, just because it was $5.

If you want an even shorter shortcut to spice blend creations, a few reputable brands of pre-made spice blends I recommend are Mountain Rose Herbs, Braggs and Mrs. Dash, in that order. So, in a pinch, go ahead and buy from those brands. Otherwise, I encourage you to create your own ready-made seasoning blends and use them regularly to add amazing flavor profiles to your healthy culinary creations. Additionally, when making spice blends, you can certainly store them in a Ziploc bag, plastic container or something similar, but I highly recommend either purchasing a spice bottle rack with glass bottles that you can fill and label, or when making larger quantities of the seasoning blends you think you'll use most regularly, go ahead and purchase some half pint mason jars and use them to store your spice blends. And remember to only make your seasoning blends in quantities that you'll use within 6 months for optimal freshness, aroma and flavor.

Easy Mediterranean Seasoning Blend

Ingredients:

4 tablespoons dried oregano

8 teaspoons dried thyme

4 teaspoons dried basil

4 teaspoons dried marjoram

4 teaspoons dried minced onion

4 teaspoons dried minced garlic

Combine all of the spices in a mixing bowl and stir until well blended. If you prefer a finer grade seasoning, give the spices a quick couple of pulses in a food processor or bullet blender. Transfer into a tightly sealed container and use within 6 months for optimal freshness. Shake well before using.

Southern Creole Seasoning Blend

Ingredients:

5 tablespoons paprika

3 tablespoons sea salt

2 tablespoons dried oregano

2 tablespoons dried basil

2 tablespoons garlic powder (NOT garlic salt)

2 tablespoons onion powder

1 tablespoon dried thyme

1 tablespoon cayenne pepper

1 tablespoon white pepper

1 tablespoon black pepper

Combine all of the spices in a mixing bowl and stir until well blended. Transfer into a tightly sealed container and use within 6 months for optimal freshness. Shake well before using.

Easy Garam Masala Indian Seasoning Blend

Ingredients:

3 tablespoons ground cumin

4-1/2 teaspoons ground black pepper

4-1/2 teaspoons ground cardamom

4-1/2 teaspoons ground coriander

1 tablespoon ground cinnamon

1-1/2 teaspoons ground nutmeg

1-1/2 teaspoons ground cloves

Combine all of the spices in a mixing bowl and stir until well blended. Transfer into a tightly sealed container and use within 6 months for optimal freshness. Shake well before using.

Cajun Seasoning Blend

Ingredients:

5 tablespoons chili powder

4 tablespoons paprika

2 tablespoons sea salt

2 tablespoons ground coriander

2 tablespoons dried oregano

4 teaspoons ground cumin

2 teaspoons black pepper

Combine all of the spices in a mixing bowl and stir until well blended. Transfer into a tightly sealed container and use within 6 months for optimal freshness. Shake well before using.

Asian Seasoning Blend

Ingredients:

6 tablespoons ground anise

3 tablespoons ground black pepper

3 tablespoons sea salt

3 tablespoons ground cinnamon

3 tablespoons ground fennel

3 tablespoons ground cloves

Combine all of the spices in a mixing bowl and stir until well blended. Transfer into a tightly sealed container and use within 6 months for optimal freshness. Shake well before using.

Classic Herbs de Provence

Ingredients:

½ cup dried thyme

¼ cup dried marjoram

2 tablespoons dried rosemary

2 tablespoons dried savory (winter or summer – may substitute with equal amount of dried sage)

2 teaspoons orange zest

1 teaspoon dried Lavender

1 teaspoon ground fennel

Combine all of the spices in a mixing bowl and stir until well blended. If you prefer a finer grade seasoning, give the spices a quick couple of pulses in a food processor or bullet blender. Transfer into a tightly sealed container and use within 6 months for optimal freshness. Shake well before using.

Chili Seasoning Blend

Ingredients:

½ cup chili powder

¼ cup garlic powder (not garlic salt)

¼ cup dried oregano

¼ cup ground cumin

3 tablespoons onion powder

1 tablespoon dried thyme

Combine all of the spices in a mixing bowl and stir until well blended. Transfer into a tightly sealed container and use within 6 months for optimal freshness. Shake well before using.

Homemade Curry Powder Seasoning

Ingredients:

½ cup ground paprika

¼ cup ground cumin

¼ cup ground turmeric

3 tablespoons ground coriander

2 tablespoons ground mustard

1 tablespoon ground fennel

1 tablespoon cardamom

1 teaspoon ground cinnamon

(optional add-ins)

2 extra tablespoons ground fennel (for added sweetness)

½ teaspoon ground cloves (to boost complex flavors)

1 teaspoon – 1 tablespoon red pepper flakes (for spicy heat)

Combine all of the spices in a mixing bowl and stir until well blended. Transfer into a tightly sealed container and use within 6 months for optimal freshness. Shake well before using.

Homemade Italian Seasoning Blend

Ingredients:

½ cup dried oregano

½ cup dried basil

½ cup dried marjoram

¼ cup dried rosemary

¼ cup dried thyme

2 tablespoons garlic powder (optional)

Combine all of the spices in a mixing bowl and stir until well blended. If you prefer a finer grade seasoning, give the spices a quick couple of pulses in a food processor or bullet blender. Transfer into a tightly sealed container and use within 6 months for optimal freshness. Shake well before using. *If you cook primarily with fresh garlic, then I recommend omitting the garlic powder in the seasoning blend.

Fajita Seasoning Blend

Ingredients:

½ cup chili powder

4 tablespoons sea salt

4 tablespoons paprika

2 tablespoons onion powder

2 tablespoons garlic powder

2 tablespoons cumin

1-2 teaspoons cayenne powder (optional)

Combine all of the spices in a mixing bowl and stir until well blended. Transfer into a tightly sealed container and use within 6 months for optimal freshness. Shake well before using.

Creole Seasoning Blend

Ingredients:

10 tablespoons paprika

6 tablespoons sea salt

4 tablespoons onion powder

4 tablespoons garlic powder

4 tablespoons dried oregano

4 tablespoons dried basil

2 tablespoons dried thyme

2 tablespoons black pepper

2 tablespoons white pepper

2 tablespoons cayenne powder

Combine all of the spices in a mixing bowl and stir until well blended. Transfer into a tightly sealed container and use within 6 months for optimal freshness. Shake well before using.

Homemade Beau Monde Seasoning Blend

Ingredients:

8 tablespoons ground black pepper

4 tablespoons ground white pepper

4 tablespoons sea salt

4 tablespoons ground cloves

4 tablespoons ground allspice

4 tablespoons ground bay leaf

4 teaspoons ground cinnamon

4 teaspoons ground nutmeg

4 teaspoons ground mace

4 teaspoons ground celery seed

Combine all of the spices in a mixing bowl and stir until well blended. Transfer into a tightly sealed container and use within 6 months for optimal freshness. Shake well before using.

Zesty Seasoning Salt Blend

Ingredients:

1-1/2 cups sea salt

½ cup black pepper

1/8 cup garlic powder

3 tablespoons onion powder

1-1/2 teaspoons cayenne powder

½ teaspoon ground ginger

Combine all of the spices in a mixing bowl and stir until well blended. Transfer into a tightly sealed container and use within 6 months for optimal freshness. Shake well before using.

Spicy Salt-Free Seasoning Blend

Ingredients:

¼ cup ground black pepper

¼ cup garlic powder

¼ cup onion powder

3 tablespoons paprika

2 tablespoons chili powder

2 tablespoons dried parsley

1 tablespoon red pepper flakes

Combine all of the spices in a mixing bowl and stir until well blended. Transfer into a tightly sealed container and use within 6 months for optimal freshness. Shake well before using.

Lemon Pepper Salt Seasoning Blend

Ingredients:

½ cup pre-dried lemon zest (ground)

6 tablespoons black pepper

5 tablespoons sea salt

Combine all of the spices in a mixing bowl and stir until well blended. If you prefer a finer grade seasoning, give the spices a quick couple of pulses in a food processor or bullet blender. Transfer into a tightly sealed container and use within 6 months for optimal freshness. Shake well before using.

Gina 'The Veggie Goddess' Matthews

BONUS CHAPTER 2: TIPS FOR A SUCCESSFUL VEGETARIAN LIFESTYLE

Gina 'The Veggie Goddess' Matthews

In this bonus chapter, I would like to address some of the most common missteps that occur when trying to convert to a healthy vegetarian or vegan lifestyle, and provide you with a comprehensive list of tips to help you easily avoid and recover from those missteps and achieve a successful vegetarian or vegan lifestyle.

If you are new to the vegetarian lifestyle it can sometimes feel overwhelming making changes, and this proves especially true the unhealthier your current dietary habits are. But, once you get familiar with some of the basics of a plant-based diet, you'll realize just how easy it really is to eat a healthy balanced meal any time of the day. Additionally, even the most seasoned vegetarian can fall off the plant-based nutrition wagon, and start injecting some unhealthy eating habits back into their diet. No matter where you fall on this spectrum, use these tips whenever needed to keep you on track with your healthy vegetarian lifestyle.

Lose the "I need to be perfect" attitude.

One of the most common factors that primes people for failure is the "I need to be perfect" attitude. Whether starting a new exercise program, a new nutrition program, and even a new hobby or career, the need to be perfect makes more people give up and quit than accepting that you're not perfect and staying committed to your goal. This puritan approach is not necessary and it is self-sabotaging. If you feel that you lean in this direction, I highly recommend keeping a notebook or calendar of some kind that you can mark down all of your successes and review them often. This is a great motivation tool for new and seasoned vegetarians alike.

Produce prepping and repurposing leftovers.

Never before has society lived in such a harried state. Juggling work, school and family, running your own business and managing other endeavours is an exhausting and seemingly never-ending way of life. While many people's intentions are to cook healthy, nature-made meals, their perpetual state of exhaustion often trumps these good intentions and they end up grabbing a fast food meal, or pre-made processed food product from the store. Neither are good options. What is a good option is making healthy, nature-made vegetarian meals that are quick and easy to prepare and two of the most important steps you can take to do that is: 1) Food prepping and 2) Repurposing leftovers.

Start by always prepping your freshly bought produce right when you bring it home from the market. While this can't be done with all produce, it definitely can be done with the most frequently used ones, such as onions, mushrooms, bell peppers, carrots, celery, broccoli, cauliflower, etc. After you put your other groceries away, give your produce a thorough wash and dry and cut them up into slices, dices or chunks. Place them into tightly sealed containers and store them in the fridge. Next, anytime you have any amount of leftover rice, beans, quinoa, pasta, etc., keep them in the fridge for a quick put-together meal. Yes, even if it's only a single spoonful of rice, beans, quinoa, etc. Now, when you're time crunched, all you have to do is assemble some of your healthy prepped and leftover foods and put them together for a quick and easy healthy vegetarian meal.

For example, beat a couple eggs together and make a southwest style omelet by adding in some of your prepped and leftover veggies, beans and/or rice, all in less than 5 minutes. Or, preheat your oven and stir together the last few days worth of leftovers in a bowl and stuff the mixture into a hollowed out bell pepper or carved out zucchini. Bake in the oven for 30-40 minutes while you're tending to something else, and before you know it, your healthy vegetarian meal is hot and ready. Another option is to stir together an assortment of prepped and/or leftover veggies, beans, rice or cooked grain into a crock pot and cook it on low during the day while you're at work or school. When you get home, your healthy vegetarian chili or stew will be warm and ready for you to serve. Prepping is essential to producing quick and easy meals, and every good restaurant in the world knows it, which is why they have a line of food prep cooks in every one of their kitchens.

Choose your kitchen appliances and gadgets wisely.

Having every cool kitchen appliance and gadget that comes along does not guarantee culinary or vegetarian diet success. How many people do you know, perhaps yourself included, have a bunch of exercise equipment lying around the house that is either collecting dust or is being used as a coat rack? Having it and using it are two very different things. I have a dedicated exercise room in my house that is filled with only the equipment that I actually use. The same goes for my kitchen. I only have appliances and gadgets that I actually use. Since I obviously don't eat meat, I do not have an outdoor grill. I do have an indoor grill, which I use to make veggie kabobs and other grilled items. I do juice regularly, therefore I also have a juicer. Remember in the previous tip covering food prepping for the purpose of making meal preparation quick and easy? Well, if you don't intend on putting the time and effort into using an appliance or gadget, and then cleaning it afterwards, then purchasing it would be a bad investment. It would be a waste of money, a waste of counter or cupboard space, and it will bring you no closer to your goal of quick and easy vegetarian meal preparation.

One of the most popular of kitchen gadget purchases that quickly gets put into the garage or sold or discarded, are the many varieties of food slicers, dicers and spiralizers. People often don't have the counter space to keep these gadgets assembled, so they must be unassembled and stored in a cabinet. Therefore, before each use they must be assembled, and then after using and cleaning, unassembled and stored back in the cabinet. This gets old fast. Far faster it would be to cut your produce then to do all this, and faster yet if you follow the tip about always food prepping. Again, buying lots of kitchen appliances and gadgets does not guarantee you a successful vegetarian lifestyle. However, if you indeed will use it and it actually does offer a convenience than that is a wise appliance or gadget purchase to make. Therefore, it will very much be an individual preference on which appliances and gadgets are helpful and necessary. That being said, here are some basics that I personally feel will help you stay on track to a lifelong healthy vegetarian lifestyle.

Quality cutting utensil set: knives, peelers, etc..

Crock pot.

Rice cooker. (I use mine to make rice, beans, lentils, quinoa, couscous and more.)

Quality blender.

Quality bullet blender kit. (chop nuts, spices, make smoothies, raw soups, dressings, gravy, and so much more)

Quality ovenware.

Quality cookware.

Quality cookie sheets.

Quality graters and microplane.

Quality garlic press.

If you are going to regularly juice, then add a quality juicer to that list. If you live in a hot climate like I do, I live in Phoenix, then a quality toaster oven would be another good investment, along with an indoor grill. Some additional recommendations, again only if you'll use them, is a wok, a salad spinner, herb scissors, and quality baking ware if you do any fair amount of baking breads and desserts.

Don't be a junk food vegetarian.

A common misstep for new vegetarians, is swapping a greasy cheeseburger for unhealthy junk food. You may claim that "it doesn't contain meat", which might be true, but those junk food choices are loaded with high fructose corn syrup, MSG, artificial flavors and colors and a boat load of other chemicals and unnatural ingredients. If you see an obese vegetarian, you can be sure their diet is high in junk food, non-meat fast food and non-meat processed food.

A healthy vegetarian lifestyle is based around plant-based nutrition, which includes fresh fruits and vegetables, whole, unprocessed grains and legumes, seeds and nuts and healthy oils. You want your food to be nature-made, not lab-made, and always in its natural state or as minimally processed as possible. This guideline extends to the many available packaged vegetarian food products that are available as well. For example; the majority of commercially prepared veggie burgers are loaded with unhealthy ingredients, including MSG. It is far better to make your own veggie burgers and keep them in the fridge or freezer for a quick and convenient meal.

Realize that your shopping habits are going to change.

Shopping for processed foods is completely opposite of shopping for nature-made and natural food items. Processed foods come with chemical preservatives, chemical colorings and chemical flavorings. They also come with genetically modified ingredients, hormones, antibiotics and artificial sweeteners. All of these components also give processed foods an incredibly unnatural shelf-life. Therefore, when shopping for these items you can overload your cart to the max because they'll last for months and even years in your pantry. On the flipside, nature-made and natural food items are highly perishable and moderately perishable. Nature-made food items have a much shorter shelf-life, which requires more frequent trips to the grocery store, natural foods store or farmers market. Remember this about food....long shelf-life equals short human life and short shelf-life equals long human life. Organic foods are even more perishable, due to their not being saturated with toxic pesticides, herbicides and insecticides. Organic is obviously what you want to strive for as much as possible, but do what you can and as often as you can within the confines of your budget. And, when purchasing conventional produce, always discard the peels and skins as this is where all those toxic residues are most concentrated and can never be fully washed off. So, frequent shopping trips in this case, is a very good thing.

Avoid eating out...yes, this includes when you are at work or school.

Unless you have a natural food market or restaurant near your work or school, I recommend avoiding eating out during your time at work or school all together. As long as you are food prepping and repurposing your leftovers to make quick and easy meals, you should always have on hand healthy vegetarian meals to bring to work or school. Planning and prepping is key and will help you avoid making unhealthy food choices when your stomach is growling and you only have 30 minutes for lunch. Purchase some containers that you can pack your homemade vegetarian meals in, and when you are cleaning up from dinner go ahead and prep your lunch for the following day. Again, always having prepped food ready and available in your fridge will make this an easy and successful part of your continued healthy vegetarian lifestyle.

Support and strengthen your vegetarian lifestyle by getting educated.

It is a gross misconception and falsely promoted fact that one needs to eat meat to be strong and healthy. I strongly urge you to become educated on such matters by watching some of the many very educational documentaries that are available on the subject matter. In fact, do NOT skip this step. You will be surprised, shocked and outraged by what you will learn. Facts that the commercial meat industry, processed food industry, pharmaceutical industry and even the western health industry does not want you to know, and they pour billions of dollars into their false marketing efforts each and every year to make sure they keep their dirty secrets hidden from the public. Here are some of the many documentaries that I recommend you watch as soon as possible. Trust me, what you will see and learn will only serve to swiftly reinforce your healthy vegetarian and vegan lifestyle.

Earthlings

Forks over Knives

Food Inc.

Food Matters

The Cove

Slaughterhouse: The Shocking Story of Greed, Neglect and Inhumane Treatment Inside the U.S. Meat Industry

Fat, Sick and Nearly Dead

Vegucated

Super Size Me

King Corn

The World According to Monsanto

Don't expect those around you to support your vegetarian lifestyle.

It's unfortunate, but oftentimes when we embark on a new venture, be it a venture to lose weight, start our own business, build our own house, or become a vegetarian or vegan, those whom we would think would be the most supportive of our efforts are often the ones who ridicule and even undermine our goals through indirect or direct behaviors on their part. It's a psychology of transference that causes these unsupportive actions and reactions. Your friends and family can sometimes not want you to succeed because they are jealous not only of your efforts, but of your potential success and realized success. Other times, your friends and family may not want you to succeed because they see it as a direct or indirect threat to their own lifestyle, habits and goals. Regardless of their reasons or their reactions, the main person's reasons and reactions that are important are yours.

For new vegetarians, I recommend finding support through like-minded friends and family if possible as well as through online resources and books and documentaries. Once you're further along in your transition to a vegetarian or vegan lifestyle, your beliefs and habits will be much more secure and you are less apt to be influenced by disingenuous behavior from others. And, all those jokes about vegetarians and vegans will just run right off of your back, like water running off of a duck's back.

Convert your favorite dishes into vegetarian versions.

Another easy transition tip from meat based meals to plant based meals, is to simply create vegetarian versions of your favorite dishes. If you enjoy a nice thick burrito, have one, just without the meat. Fill it with rice, beans and your favorite veggies and serve it with salsa, fresh chopped cilantro and fresh lime wedges. If you like lasagna, just replace the meat with extra veggies. If you like eggs and sausage for breakfast, swap out the sausage for some sautéed mushrooms or diced eggplant. In most cases, just enjoying your favorite dishes without the meat is good enough. In other cases, you can just swap out the meat component with a healthy non-meat alternative. Make a crock pot of chili filled with beans and variety of diced veggies. Make stir fries with extra veggies. And, remember to not sabotage your efforts by replacing meat with junk food.

Transitioning, detoxing, awakening and aligning to a healthier you.

Typically when people eat an unhealthy western diet loaded with junk food, meat and processed foods, their taste buds have been desensitized to what real food tastes like. Additionally, their bodies acquire real addictions to the chemicals that are saturating the unhealthy foods that they eat. This will take your body and taste buds some time to detox and recover from. Yes, as you transition into a healthy, plant-based vegetarian diet you literally will be detoxing from these substances. And, as your body starts to purge itself of these stored toxins you will likely feel worse before you feel better as they are expelled from your body via all of the elimination pathways of your body. This is expected and normal. This is NOT an indicator that your vegetarian or vegan diet is making you ill. It IS an indicator that your body is cleansing itself of stored toxins from your previously unhealthy diet. This transition is temporary.

As you replace more and more of those unhealthy foods with nature-made foods, your taste buds will awaken to what REAL food tastes like. Your body will start purging all those stored toxins, excess weight and cellulite. Your body's chemistry will start to balance and align itself, ridding you of many if not all of those imbalances that your may be experiencing. You will feel lighter, and you will actually be lighter. Your mind will gain new clarity and focus, your mood will improve and your energy levels will surge. Your skin will take on a healthier glow, and your hair and nails will strengthen and grow faster. Your ability to exercise will increase. Your sleep patterns will greatly improve. Your confidence will soar, and you will be a walking testament to the many positive aspects of a plant-based, vegetarian lifestyle.

I can't tell you how many people who used to give me a hard time about my vegetarian lifestyle in my younger years now comment on how healthy I am, and how I don't look near my biological years, and I have two grown children and three grandchildren. This can happen for you too, and it is never too early to start, and it is never too late to start. A healthy vegetarian or vegan lifestyle is easy to follow, and the rewards are enormous. Natural body weight maintenance, anti-aging benefits (physical and mental), extraordinary immune system defenses and incredible health are all yours.

I hope that you find great value in these tips for a successful vegetarian lifestyle as well as all of the recipes contained in this book. I am extremely passionate about plant-based nutrition and a clean, green, organic lifestyle. After all, nature-made food is meant to be our body's medicine, not pharmaceuticals.

Bon Veggie Appetit!

Gina "The Veggie Goddess" Matthews

AVAILABLE BOOKS BY AUTHOR:

Easy Vegetarian Cooking: 100 – 5 Ingredients or Less, Easy & Delicious Vegetarian Recipes

Natural Foods: 100-5- Ingredients or Less, Raw Food Recipes for Every Meal Occasion

Easy Vegetarian Cooking: 75 Delicious Vegetarian Casserole Recipes

Easy Vegetarian Cooking: 75 Delicious Vegetarian Soup and Stew Recipes

The Veggie Goddess Vegetarian Cookbook Collection: Volumes 1-4

Easy Vegan Cooking: 100 Easy and Delicious Vegan Recipes

Vegan Cooking: 50 Delectable Vegan Dessert Recipes

Holiday Vegan Recipes: Holiday Menu Planning

for Halloween through New Years

The Veggie Goddess Vegan Cookbook Collection: Volumes 1-3

Natural Cures: 200 All Natural Fruit & Veggie Remedies for Weight Loss, Health and Beauty

Healthy Living: How to Purify Your Body in a Polluted World

Gluten Free Bread: 100 Wheat-Free Bread and Baked Goods Recipes

100 – 5 Ingredients or Less Quick and Easy Vegetarian Recipes (Volume 2)

Cooking Notes:

Cooking Notes:

Cooking Notes:

Cooking Notes:

100 – 5 Ingredients or Less Quick & Easy Vegetarian Recipes
(Volume 2)

Cooking Notes:

Gina 'The Veggie Goddess' Matthews

ABOUT THE AUTHOR:

Gina 'The Veggie Goddess' Matthews, resides in sunny Phoenix, Arizona, and has been a lover of animals, nature, gardening, natural living and, of course, vegetarian and vegan cuisine since childhood. 'The Veggie Goddess' strongly encourages home gardening, supporting your local farmers and organic food co-ops, preserving the well-being of Mother Earth, and supporting and protecting animal rights.

http://www.theveggiegoddess.com

http://www.facebook.com/theveggiegoddess

http://www.pinterest.com/veggiegoddess

Gina 'The Veggie Goddess' Matthews

Made in the USA
San Bernardino, CA
19 August 2018